Complete
INDIAN
Cookbook

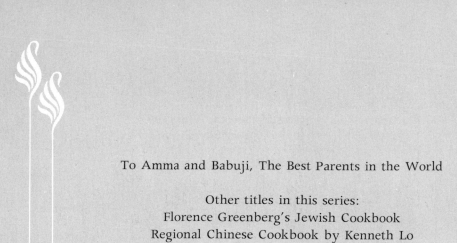

To Amma and Babuji, The Best Parents in the World

Complete
INDIAN
Cookbook

Michael Pandya

Hamlyn
London · New York · Sydney · Toronto

Acknowledgements

I wish to record my grateful thanks to everyone who offered me their constructive criticisms and invaluable advice in the preparation of this book. In particular, I would like to thank Lala and Kallu, the best chaat makers in my world, for sharing with me some of their secrets of many scrumptious savouries. Thanks also to Auntie Taoosi, a friend of the family, for allowing me a peep or two into the cuisine of the Moghuls and the Nawabs.

Moving now to my own family circle, I am most indebted to Chhoti mami, my Jaipuri aunt, for our parleys on her vegetarian wizardry. It is a pity I still do not know the secret of all that taste in her hands. Also precious to me, was the help of my Mausi, my mother's sister, who delighted me with her massive methodology on the Indian pickles; my sisters, Jiya and Munni, who overwhelmed me by unearthing the width and volume of our family's culinary artistry; and of Mamma, my mother-in-law, who despite her reluctance, let slip the mysteries of her kitchen delights – I did not even have to use my personal charm and persuasion to melt her!

I am pleased with my children – Mohit, Manoj, Pawan and Peeyush – who made no mean contribution towards accomplishing those little but important things that have got to be done in getting a manuscript ready for the publisher. However, my mainstay for this book, as for my earlier publications, was my wife, Preeti. She was there whenever she was needed, always smiling. To her, what can I say but 'thank you'!

I am much obliged to my brother – Avadhesh, my cousin Birjan bhaisaheb, and my brother-in-law – Raju, for saving me a good deal of time during my recent visit to India by organising all my internal flights, train reservations and car journeys; for taking notes and recording discussions; and also for taking me out to the best hotels and restaurants wherever I went, in order for me to note the contemporary trends in the Indian eating habits.

Congratulations are due to The Hamlyn Group for their competent handling of this publication and I must also express my gratitude for the cosy cooperation and alacritous assistance meted out to me by their staff, in general, and by Jane Todd, their cookery editor, in particular. Who knows at this point in time as to what will come out of this association?

Photography by Mick Dean
Line illustrations by Marilyn Day

Published by
The Hamlyn Publishing Group Limited
London · New York · Sydney · Toronto
Astronaut House, Feltham, Middlesex, England
© Copyright The Hamlyn Publishing Group Limited 1980
Reprinted 1981
ISBN 0 600 34918 7

Phototypeset by Servis Filmsetting Limited, Manchester
Printed in Singapore

Contents

Useful facts and figures

Notes on metrication

In this book quantities are given in metric and Imperial measures. Exact conversion from Imperial to metric measures does not usually give very convenient working quantities and so the metric measures have been rounded off into units of 25 grams. The table below shows the recommended equivalents.

Ounces	Approx g to nearest whole figure	Recommended conversion to nearest unit of 25
1	28	25
2	57	50
3	85	75
4	113	100
5	142	150
6	170	175
7	198	200
8	227	225
9	255	250
10	283	275
11	312	300
12	340	350
13	368	375
14	396	400
15	425	425
16 (1 lb)	454	450
17	482	475
18	510	500
19	539	550
20 (1¼ lb)	567	575

Note: When converting quantities over 20 oz first add the appropriate figures in the centre column, then adjust to the nearest unit of 25. As a general guide, 1 kg (1000 g) equals 2.2 lb or about 2 lb 3 oz. This method of conversion gives good results in nearly all cases, although in certain pastry and cake recipes a more accurate conversion is necessary to produce a balanced recipe.

Liquid measures The millilitre has been used in this book and the following table gives a few examples.

Imperial	Approx ml to nearest whole figure	Recommended ml
¼ pint	142	150 ml
½ pint	283	300 ml
¾ pint	425	450 ml
1 pint	567	600 ml
1½ pints	851	900 ml
1¾ pints	992	1000 ml (1 litre)

Spoon measures All spoon measures given in this book are level unless otherwise stated.
Can sizes At present, cans are marked with the exact (usually to the nearest whole number) metric equivalent of the Imperial weight of the contents, so we have followed this practice when giving can sizes.

Oven temperatures

The table below gives recommended equivalents.

	°C	°F	Gas Mark
Very cool	110	225	$\frac{1}{4}$
	120	250	$\frac{1}{2}$
Cool	140	275	1
	150	300	2
Moderate	160	325	3
	180	350	4
Moderately	190	375	5
hot	200	400	6
Hot	220	425	7
	230	450	8
Very hot	240	475	9

Notes for American and Australian users

In America the 8-oz measuring cup is used. In Australia metric measures are now used in conjunction with the standard 250-ml measuring cup. The Imperial pint, used in Britain and Australia, is 20 fl oz, while the American pint is 16 fl oz. It is important to remember that the Australian tablespoon differs from both the British and American tablespoons; the table below gives a comparison. The British standard tablespoon, which has been used throughout this book, holds 17.7 ml, the American 14.2 ml, and the Australian 20 ml. A teaspoon holds approximately 5 ml in all three countries.

British	American	Australian
1 teaspoon	1 teaspoon	1 teaspoon
1 tablespoon	1 tablespoon	1 tablespoon
2 tablespoons	3 tablespoons	2 tablespoons
$3\frac{1}{2}$ tablespoons	4 tablespoons	3 tablespoons
4 tablespoons	5 tablespoons	$3\frac{1}{2}$ tablespoons

NOTE: WHEN MAKING ANY OF THE RECIPES IN THIS BOOK, ONLY FOLLOW ONE SET OF MEASURES AS THEY ARE NOT INTERCHANGEABLE.

Introduction

When other people write books, they wipe the dust from the volumes in archives, burn midnight oil shuffling the pages of books in the libraries, subscribe to journals and conduct interviews. When I embarked on the venture, I took a holiday and went to India to meet my people – I had long discussions with them and extracted further gems in the Indian cuisine to add to my collection in the process.

I am lucky to hail from a family of excellent cooks and lovers of good food. My mother was an extremely good cook and a true goddess of our home. That was my introduction to the Indian cuisine. In addition, my sisters and aunts have taste in their hands which apparently rubs off on the dishes they make. This is another mystery of the Orient: two people start to make a dish with identical ingredients and use the same methods, but the final results are never the same!

Almost none of my people can tell you the exact weight or measurement of ingredients to be used. This indeed is the case with most traditional artistes of Indian cuisine; they guess the quantities and get perfect results every time. However, I would suggest that you stick to the specifications of the recipes for now and discard your kitchen scales only when you fancy yourself to be a true expert.

Indian food is already very popular in the West. In the United Kingdom, the existence of a large Indian population, an avalanche of the Indian restaurants all over the place, coupled with Britain's long association with India, have combined to give a further fillip to the already considerable interest in Indian food that exists in the indigenous population and has aroused people's curiosity.

Indian cookery as we see it today is the quintessence of the cooking techniques of numerous nationalities and civilisations connected with India for more than a thousand years. Indian food is beautiful to behold and pleases the palate. It is good for the body and mind and is an experience to cherish. Ingredients like khoya, paneer, ghee, garam masala and the like make Indian cookery unique in the world.

The spices used for making Indian food make it what it is. It is wrong to think that Indian food should always be 'hot'; too many hot spices burn the palate and tend to upset the tummy, in addition to making your tongue skinless. Not all spices are hot in themselves; it is the chillies and pepper or the combined effect of the spices that provide the pungency and the 'kick' to the dishes.

India has for long stood as the undisputed centre of vegetarianism. Many factors have been responsible for this phenomenon. The Hindus are by religion forbidden to eat meat, Purely for economical reasons also, they can not do anything else. They cannot afford to buy meat, so are content to be vegetarians. The vegetarian dishes supply all the proteins and vitamins that a human body needs. Indians are peaceful people and abhor the horrors of killing, even animals. Thus, on humanitarian grounds also, vegetarianism has large support in India.

The non-vegetarian part of the Indian culinary art consists of dishes that are tender and juicy. The dainties and delicacies made with lamb, mutton, beef, pork, duck and chicken are part and parcel of non-vegetarian cookery. Contrary to the mistaken belief, not all the non-vegetarian food from India is curry. Curry is the name given to a group of delectable dishes, prepared in many different ways, producing many different tastes and flavours. In this sense curries are like wines; they may look the same or similar, but they are so different!

It may not be possible for you to cook these dishes every day. Indeed it is not advisable to do so, because then you will become insensitive to the aroma and flavour of the Indian food and the sense of novelty and excitement would be gone. Cook them for variety: variety is the spice of life, as they say. Have a spicy, juicy life!

Each region has its peculiar features and they all lend variety, richness and a character to the Indian cuisine.

From the northern region come the Kashmiri and Punjabi styles of cooking. Kashmiri cooking has a lot of character of its own. Also influenced by the Moghuls, this blending of the two styles has produced a grand new world of cookery. Kashmiris have perfected the art of meat frying and producing truly heavenly curries without using thickening agents such as onion and garlic.

The Punjabis are some of the best cooks in the country and are known gourmets. The Punjab is the home of tandoori cooking and there are as many varieties of parauntha as there are states in India. Punjab is also famous for many other sweetmeats and delicacies. Punjabis are basically wheat eaters and do not eat much rice.

The southern Indians are quite the opposite. South India is a strong-hold of the Hindus and vegetable dishes and rice are their staple foods. They make many varieties of vegetable dishes, like aviyal, and use mustard oil as their cooking medium. Coconut and coconut milk and also tamarind in various forms are used for cooking. South Indian curries are thin and fiery, such as the vindaloo dishes. Paper-thin papads are also a speciality of south India.

Moving East, you see Bengal and Bihar. Being surrounded by the rivers and the seas, fish is cheap and in plentiful supply. Not surprisingly, therefore, fish is widely eaten here and rice is another integral part of the diet. The peculiar features of this region's cookery are many. Most of the cooking here is done in mustard oil, which gives a special taste and flavour to the dishes. For spicing their food, the mustard, cumin, anise and fenugreek seeds are their 'hot' favourites. The Easterners excel in making stupendous sweetmeats and savouries.

The cuisine of the Western regions comes mainly from Goa and Bombay. Goan food is usually hot, using a lot of coconut milk, boiled into thick or thin gravies and tamarind juice, as in South India. Spices here are usually ground before use and the more delectable a dish, the longer it takes to cook. The popular dishes of the cosmopolitan Bombay region are kulfi, golgappa or the various sharbats which are roughly the same as elsewhere.

The cuisine of central India has elan and a definite style. Everything cooked in this region is dominated by the Moghul style of cooking, which is well advanced in expertise and finesse. The Indian cooking, particularly the meat dishes, attained new heights during the Moghul period.

Choose your dishes from everywhere and try to blend the regional dishes into cosmopolitan ones. Most of the dishes given in this book are just that, and I suggest that you begin with those. Then start experimenting, if you wish.

When dealing with the Indian dishes, do not economise on time, be it in cooking or eating them. Eat in a relaxed and unhurried way in convivial company. Meet, greet and treat the dishes as a lover does the beloved. The consummation of the eating act is a physical phenomenon which has a salubrious effect on your health and happiness. You will be rejuvenated and a new gust of life will tingle through your veins. You will feel like a new person. If this is not heaven, what is?

There is a belief amongst Indian food lovers that the spicy and exotic food makes you sexy and virile. An example given in this connection is Lord Krishna of India who, it is claimed, had some 16000 wives and uncounted casual and serious girl-friends. All the virility and youth of Krishna – and he must have had plenty of both – must have come from his food. It will be a hard job for anyone to equal that record, let alone exceed it! Make and eat the dishes from this book to find out what Indian food can do for you.

I have already taken too much of your time, just chatting about Indian food, and do not wish to stand between you and the exotic food a moment longer. Bon appetit!

Michael Pandya

The armoury of an Indian kitchen

There are certain utensils and other tools which you will find in all traditional Indian kitchens. Whilst it is true that most of these are particularly suitable for making Indian dishes, the western counterparts do just as well in making the same dishes. In some instances, western tools may even be better. A wooden spatula is far better, as stirrers go, than a metallic karchhi or chamchaa. This is so because, not only do the metallic spoons burn your fingers, they in fact destroy the taste and flavour of the spices.

Although it is advisable to avoid the contact of metals with spices, it is not to say that all metals are inimical to Indian food; Stainless steel and enamelware are quite acceptable and widely used.

In order to create a total Indian ambience in your kitchen, I suggest you use typical Indian utensils – I give below the names and descriptions of a few more commonly used items.

Chakla-belan A wooden rolling board and rolling pin used to roll out thin discs made from dough and pastry.

Chamchaa A scoop used for serving soups and curries. Resembles a ladle.

Chimtaa Long, flat tongs with blunt edges, useful for making chapatis.

Chulhaa A half-moon shaped hearth, found in most houses in the Uttar Pradesh area. Using coal or wood as fuel, these are used for making chapatis and some minor baking and roasting.

Jhannaa A spoon with a long handle and a perforated disc at the end for making batter drops.

Kadhai A deep, wide-mouthed metal pan with handles on both sides. Made of iron, brass or stainless steel, it is used for deep frying and the making of dishes such as halwas.

Karchhi A spoon with a long handle and a flat disc at the end of it. It is used as a stirrer and for pressing down things like papad to facilitate their proper cooking.

Katori A small bowl made of metal, used for each curry dish per meal per person.

Imamdusta and daanti A pestle and mortar made of enamel or clay. For pounding harder ingredients, a khalla and musaria made of cast iron are used.

Seekh A long metal rod (about 5 mm/$\frac{1}{4}$ inch thick) with a tapering end. Kababs and tikkas are threaded on to this rod and are roasted on an open fire.

Sil-batta A sil is a large, stone slab, measuring about 15 × 30 cm/6 × 12 inches and a batta measures about 5 × 10 cm/2 × 4 inches. The surface of the sil is rough and spices and herbs are ground by placing them on the sil and pressing the batta against them.

Tandoor A clay oven for baking the Indian breads and meat dishes.

Tawa A circular, metal plate, usually made of iron, with a handle. It is usually used for making chapatis and paraunthas.

Thaali A metal platter or salver with a low rim, used with katoris for serving a traditional meal.

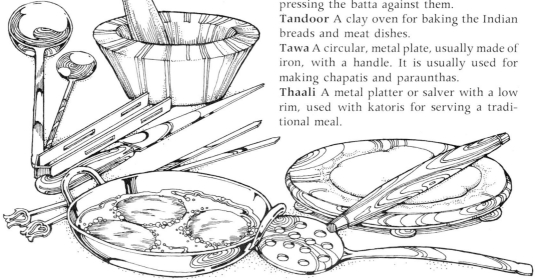

10

Useful tips for the uninitiated

Salt You should always adjust the quantities to your personal taste and liking.

Chillies and black pepper It is better to err on the side of caution and reduce the quantity of chillies and black peppers in all the dishes you cook. If the dish is not pungent enough for you, more chilli can always be added.

Whole spices These are always hotter than their powdered equivalents. As for chillies and pepper, reduce the quantities of specified amounts until you find your level of acceptance.

Adding water to frying spices When you are adding water to the sizzling spices in a pan, remove the pan from the heat first. Pour the water slowly from the edges of the pan, lest the spices spit up into your face.

Fish without a fishy smell Prepare a paste with 2 tablespoons chick pea flour, 1 teaspoon turmeric powder, 1 teasooon salt and 4 tablespoons water. Rub this paste over the fish and leave for about 30 minutes. Then wash the fish thoroughly under cold running water. The fishy smell will have gone and you can cook it as prescribed.

The addition of yogurt When yogurt is added to various dishes, it should be whipped or at least beaten a little before use.

The frying of cumin and mustard seeds When frying either of these, cover the pan to prevent spitting.

Pots and pans The contact of metal and spices should be avoided as far as possible, so use stainless steel, enamelware and wooden spoons. Cook dishes with a high acid content in earthenware pots or non-stick pans.

The quantity of spices and garlic I suggest you experiment with smaller quantities of these ingredients if you are not yet accustomed to Indian flavours, but always use them in the correct proportions, one to another, as prescribed in the recipe.

Menu for a meal

Traditionally, an Indian meal simply starts with all the dishes together and finishes with fresh fruit. The serving of paan is the formal conclusion of a meal. A paan is a leaf heaped with chopped betel nuts and other scented ingredients and is served folded up and secured with a clove.

The usual drink at the end of a meal is water. Wines are not normally drunk then, but champagne goes with any meal! I would, however, advise against sweet drinks and powerful liquors because they will surely destroy and drown the flavour of the food. An Indian meal can be vegetarian or non-vegetarian. Vegetarian meals can be of two types, namely kachcha or pukka. A pukka meal denotes an element of formality and the kachcha meal is one of more intimacy.

It may be useful to know that most Indian dishes can be cooked in advance and served by reheating just a few minutes before serving. Traditionally, food is served on a thali or a salver with the necessary number of bowls.

You can make your table look unusual by using red radishes instead of the usual white variety in raitas and salads.

Make shaped eggs by filling moulds with raw eggs and baking them. Used these sliced to garnish the dishes.

Since time immemorial, the main ingredients of Indian dishes have been spices, milk products and fresh fruits. It was the spices which initially attracted the British and other Europeans to India. The resultant British rule in India, stretching over some two hundred years, was bound to bring the British in close touch with the Indian cuisine. Their taste buds having been opened by the delicious and exotic Indian dishes, the British demand for Indian food in Britain was inevitable.

Vegetarian menus

(*Kachcha*)
Cauliflower soup
Chapati
Boiled rice
Toor dall
Fried okra
Stuffed aubergines
Papad
Lemon pickle in vinegar
Banana satsuma pudding
Paan

(*Pukka*)
Pumpkin soup
Puri stuffed with dall
Jackfruit curry or
Marrow kofta curry
Flattened artichokes
Papad
Batterdrop raita
Milk sweetmeat
Green cardamom, desiccated
coconut and cloves

Ginger soup
Gram flour chapati
Boiled rice
Urad dall
Minced peas
Fenugreek leaves and potatoes
Papad
Chick chops
Makhana pudding
Fried fennel with sugar candy

Vegetarian minestrone soup
Layered parauntha
Whole cauliflower
Stuffed bitter gourd
Gooseberry chutney
Cream cheese balls in syrup
Scented chopped betel nuts,
cloves and aniseed

Non-Vegetarian menus

Meat soup
Tandoori chicken
Beef kofta curry
Batter drop raita
Chilli pickle in lemon juice
Kulfi for the princes
Paan

Non-vegetarian mulligatawny soup
Prawn pullao
Minced beef curry
Bombay duck bullets
Grilled drumsticks
Chilli pickle in lemon juice
Batter coils in syrup
Paan with foil

Chicken soup
Naan
Mutton curry
Skewer kababs
Marrow raita
Coconut pudding
Green cardamom and cloves

Spin-bone soup
Mutton pullao
Nargisi kofta curry
Lovers' nuggets
Papad
Green chillies and root ginger in
lemon juice
Whitegourd sweetmeat
Roasted fennel, desiccated coconut
and green cardamom

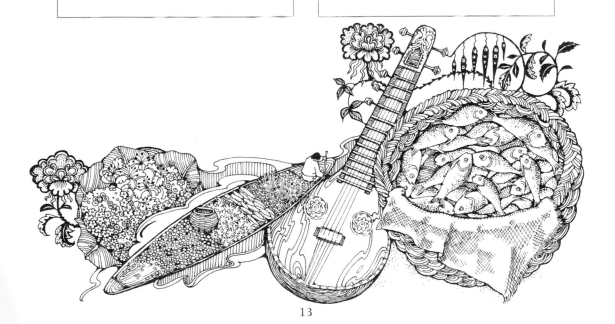

Presentation

However delicious, sustaining or wholesome a dish may be, unless it looks fetching, people will go off it even before they start. By the same token, if the goodies-laden dining table is the cynosure of all eyes in the dining hall and the aroma of the food is tantalising, chances are that even those who are not hungry would be tempted to sample your dishes.

I give below a few suggestions for making your table look more attractive. Make a feature of your dining table, rather than treating it as an object just to place food on.

Arrange fresh flowers and light up a few joss-sticks (agar batti) at least half an hour before your guests are due to arrive. Arrange the napkins in the glasses in the shape of flowers and play suitable music while eating is in progress.

Serve desserts and puddings in coloured glass bowls which will contrast with the colour of the food. Tangy puddings can be served another way. Take medium oranges or satsumas, slice each one across, making the top part smaller than the bottom. Scoop out the flesh and use the skin as bowls for serving banana-satsuma pudding, for instance.

On sizzling summer afternoons when you want to serve either sweet or sour drinks, take out a small amount of the prepared drink and freeze it as ice cubes, to serve with the drink.

The serving of soups can be simple too. Make some sippets or croûtons and keep them handy in an airtight container. Serve these croûtons with each helping or add a spoonful of fresh cream to each individual bowl.

Serve your fruit in an interesting way. Take a melon and cut it into four or more slices, discarding the seeds. In the four boat-shaped slices, cut a little depression in the fruit and fill it with syrup and fresh cream. Chill before serving. You could also dress up bananas. Peel and split them lengthwise and prop them up on a plate to resemble a boat, using cocktail sticks. Pour over some whipped yogurt and dot the surface with powdered saffron. Chill before serving.

Dishes like raitas can be served in a pineapple. Halve the fruit and scoop out the flesh. Fill the skin with the raita, cover the top and present it as a serving dish on the table.

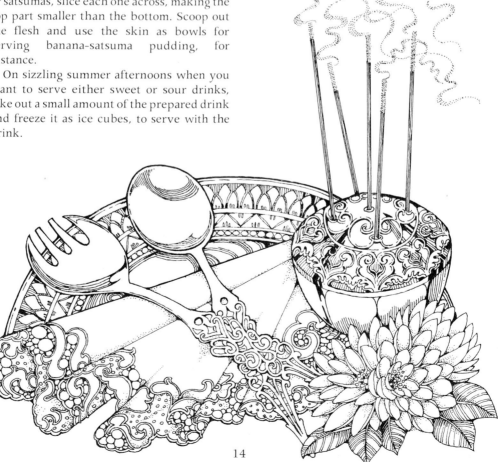

Glossary of Indian foods

English name	Hindustani name	Qualities and usage
Almond	Badaam	A nut used in sweetmeats, rich in iron and protein
Aniseed	Saunf	An appetiser used in wines and cooked dishes
Arrowroot	Araarut	A nutritious starch used in sweetmeats and faluda
Artichoke	Arbi/ghuiyan	A starchy vegetable served fried and curried
Asafoetida	Heeng	A sour digestive spice with a strong aroma
Aubergine	Baigan/brinjal	A vegetable containing iron
Baking powder	Khane ka soda	A raising agent used in pastries and batters
Banana	Kela	Used in raitas and puddings, rich in vitamins
Bay leaf	Tej patta	A herb with preservative and germicidal properties
Beef	Gaay ka gosht	A protein-rich meat used in curries and kababs
Bitter gourd	Karela	A green vegetable, rich in iron, good for the blood
Black beans	Urad ki dall	Rich in protein and iron, used in purées
Black peppercorns	Gol mirch	A digestive spice rich in vitamin C, also used ground
Bone	Haddi	Rich in calcium with nourishing marrow
Brain	Bheja	Rich in protein and phosphorus, used in curries
Butter	Makhkhan	A fat rich in vitamins A and D, used to make ghee
Buttermilk	Mattha	A light digestive drink
Cabbage	Bundgobhi	Low in calories rich in vitamin C
Capsicum	Shimla mirch	Rich in vitamin C, serve stuffed or curried
Caraway seeds	Kala zeera	A carminative and aromatic spice
Cardamom, brown	Bari illaichi	A fragrant spice with germicidal properties
Cardamom, green	Chhoti illaichi	A digestive spice used in curries and sweetmeats
Carom seeds	Ajwain	A digestive spice used as a seasoning
Carrot	Gajar	Rich in vitamin A, good for the sight
Cashew nut	Kaju	Rich in protein and vitamin B, used in sweetmeats

English name	Hindustani name	Qualities and usage
Cauliflower	Gobhi	Rich in vitamins and calcium, often cooked whole
Chapati flour	Roti ka atta	A wholesome and sustaining starch
Chicken	Murghi	Rich in protein, cooked into many dishes
Chick pea	Kabuli chanaa	Rich in iron, used in curries and stuffings
Chick pea flour	Besan	Used in snacks and many other dishes
Chilli, green	Hari mirch	Rich in vitamin C, adds a spicy flavour to food
Chilli, red	Laal mirch	A hot spice, used both whole and powdered
Chironji nut	Chiraunji	Used in puddings and desserts
Cinnamon	Daal cheeni	Strong germicidal spice used in stick or powder form
Citric acid	Neebu ka sat	A sour powder containing vitamin C
Cloves	Laung	An antiseptic spice for sweet and savoury dishes
Coconut	Nariyal	An oily fruit used in curries and sweetmeats
Coriander leaves	Dhania ki patti	An aromatic herb often used for garnishing
Coriander seeds	Dhania ke beej	A carminative and medicinal spice
Cornflour	Makka ka atta	A thickening agent used for breads and pastries
Cream cheese	Paneer/chhena	Rich in vitamins B and D, used in sweet and savoury dishes
Cucumber	Kheera/kakdi	A cooling vegetable used in raitas
Cumin seeds, black	Kala zeera	A digestive spice which reduces flatulence
Cumin seeds, white	Safed zeera	A spice used for flavouring and preserving
Curd	Dahi	Used in many dishes, has good digestive properties
Curry leaves	Meethi neem ki patti	Aromatic leaves used for flavouring
Curry powder	Garam masala	A mixture of spices with a powerful flavour
Date, dried	Chhohaaraa	An iron-rich fruit used in sonth and sweetmeats
Desiccated coconut	Sookhi garee	Used in sweetmeats and in curries
Drumsticks	Murghi ki taangen	Used in both tandoori and curried dishes
Dry red chilli	Sookhi mirch	Adds a spicy kick to curries and dry dishes

English name	Hindustani name	Qualities and usage
Duck	Batakh	An oily meat, rich in protein
Egg	Andaa	Rich in vitamins A and B, often curried
Fennel	Moti saunf	An after dinner refresher, used in pickles
Fenugreek, leaves	Methi ka saag	Rich in vitamin C and iron, used in bhaji
Fenugreek, seeds	Methi ke beej	Rich in iron, strong flavour – use sparingly
Fish	Machhli/machchhi	Rich in calcium, protein and phosphorus
Flour, wheat	Maidaa	Starch used in breads savouries and sweetmeats
Garlic	Lahsun	Strong in flavour, rich in iron, good for the blood
Ghee	Ghee	Highest quality cooking fat, made from butter
Ginger, dry	Sonth	A carminative spice used in sweet and savoury dishes
Ginger, root	Adrak	Used to flavour curries, wines and other dishes
Gold foil	Sone ka warq	A decorative digestive, used in sweet dishes
Green beans	Moong ki dall	Protein-rich pulses used in dall dishes
Green chilli	Hari mirch	Used to add spicy flavour to dishes
Green mango	Amchoor	Available as powder or pieces to give flavour
Green peas	Hari matar	Protein-rich pulse used in many dishes
Ice	Baraf	Used as a cooler in drinks
Jackfruit	Kathal	A seasonal vegetable with a delicious taste
Jaggery	Gur	Unrefined palm sugar, used in pickles
Ladyfingers	Bhindi	A tasty green vegetable, rich in vitamins
Lamb	Chhoti bhedi ka gosht	Protein-rich meat widely used for curries
Lemon	Neebu	Rich in vitamin C, used for souring
Lentils	Masoor ki dall	Protein rich pulses, used in purées and stuffings
Lime paste	Khanewala choona	A tenderising agent, often served on betel leaves
Mace	Javitri	A sedative and carminative spice
Mango	Aam	Rich in protein, used in different forms

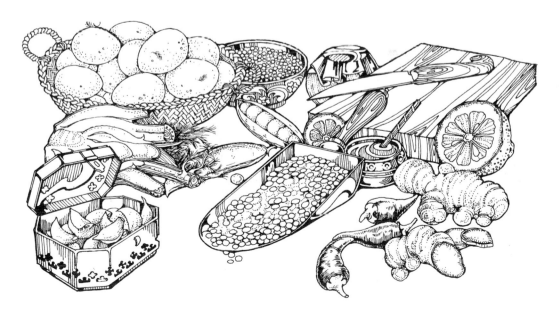

English name	Hindustani name	Qualities and usage
Marrow	Lauki	Rich in vitamins and minerals
Meat	Gosht	Often goat or lamb, excellent for curries
Milk	Doodh	Rich in calcium, protein and vitamins A and B
Mint	Podina ki patti	An aromatic herb used in chutneys and raitas
Molasses	Gur	See jaggery
Mustard oil	Sarson ka tel	Pungent cooking medium, contains vitamin D
Mustard seed	Sarson/rai	Pungent in flavour, contains manganese and vitamin D
Mutton	Bari bhed ka gosht	Rich in proteins, very suitable for curries
Nigella	Kalaunji	A seed used in pickles and stuffed vegetables
Nutmeg	Jaiphal	A digestive used in cordials, reduces flatulence
Okra	Bhindi	See ladyfingers
Onion	Pyaaz	Contains vitamin D, sulphur, used for flavouring
Orange	Santara	Rich in vitamins A and C, used in drinks and desserts
Paprika	Bari hari mirch	Spice used in curries, good for skin and digestion
Parsley	Ajmooda ki patti	A garnishing herb
Peas	Hari matar	See green peas
Pepper	Kali mirch	A spice which cools by causing perspiration
Pickle	Achaar	An accompaniment for bland foods
Pigeon pea	Arhar ki dall	A pulse used in dalls, also called toor dall
Pineapple	Anannas	Rich in vitamins A and C, often served in drinks
Pistachios	Pishta	Rich in vitamin B, used in sweetmeats
Pomegranate	Anardana	Sharp seeds used in snacks and stuffings
Poppy seeds	Khas khas	An aromatic spice, rich in protein
Pork	Suwar ka gosht	Protein-rich meat, taboo for muslims
Potato	Aloo	Carbohydrate-rich vegetable with many uses
Prawn	Jheenga machhli	An expensive delicacy, rich in protein
Preserve	Murabba	A sweetmeat which can be stored

English name	Hindustani name	Qualities and usage
Pulses	Dall	Rich in protein, a must in vegetarian meals
Pumpkin	Kaddu	Vitamin-rich, often cooked in dry bhaji
Radish	Mooli	A tangy root used in salads and bhaji
Raisins	Munaqqa	Rich in iron, used in sweet and savoury dishes
Rice	Chaawal	Rich in carbohydrates, used in pullaos and biriyani
Rice flour	Chaawal ka atta	A popular south Indian thickening agent
Rose essence	Gulab ka sat	Used in sweetmeats and puddings, a fragrant essence
Rose water	Gulab jal	An aromatic liquid used in sharbats and sweetmeats
Saffron	Kesar	A flavouring and colouring spice
Sago	Saboodaanaa	Light granular starch, used in puddings
Salt, black	Kala namak	Used in raitas and sauces, an unusual flavour
Semolina	Sooji	A thickening starch, very light on the digestion
Silver foil	Chaandi ka warq	A digestive edible foil used for decoration
Soup	Rasaa	A light starter course, introduced by the English
Spices	Masaale	A wide range of flavouring and seasoning agents
Spinach	Palak	Rich in iron, vitamins A and C and calcium
Sugar candy	Misri	Used in sweetmeats or served after a meal
Sultanas	Kishmish	Iron-rich fruit, used in sweetmeats and puddings
Tamarind	Imli	Adds piquancy to dishes
Tomato	Tamatar	Rich in vitamins A, B and C, used whole or puréed
Toor dall	Arhar ki dall	Popular pulse used in dall dishes
Turmeric	Haldi	A colouring and flavouring spice, good for the skin
Vermicelli	Semaian	A flour-based pasta, used in puddings
Vinegar	Sirka	A sour pickling agent and preservative
Whitegourd	Petha	Type of pumpkin, often used in sweetmeats
Yam	Arbi/ghuiyan	See artichoke
Yogurt	Dahi	A digestive milk product used in various dishes

Basic spices and ingredients

Garam masala
Hot spice powder

Garam masala is a mixture of several hot spices, ground together, and is the life-blood of all the major savoury dishes in an Indian meal. It is used in most curried, dry or braised dishes at various stages in the cooking. Ready-made garam masala is sold in all the Asian grocery shops, but it's not the same as your own.

METRIC/IMPERIAL	AMERICAN
15 g/½ oz black cumin seeds	1½ tablespoons black cumin seeds
15 g/½ oz white cumin seeds	1½ tablespoons white cumin seeds
75 g/3 oz coriander seeds	½ cup coriander seeds
40 g/1½ oz brown cardamom seeds	4 tablespoons brown cardamom seeds
4 bay leaves	4 bay leaves
50 g/2 oz cloves	6 tablespoons cloves
50 g/2 oz black peppercorns	¾ cup black peppercorns
15 g/½ oz grated nutmeg	2 tablespoons grated nutmeg
15 g/½ oz blade mace	1½ tablespoons blade mace
40 g/1½ oz cinnamon stick	1½ oz cinnamon stick

Roast all the ingredients together in a moderate oven (160°C, 325°F, Gas Mark 3) until they give off a strong and aromatic smell, about 10 minutes.
  When roasted, grind the spices, about one quarter at a time. If an electric grinder is not available, grind by hand and press through a fine sieve afterwards. Store in airtight containers for up to 3 months. Make sure you always close the lid tightly after use.

Vindaloo masala
Vindaloo powder

This powder is a must for vindaloo lovers, a spoonful of this in your favourite vindaloo dish will do wonders for your taste buds!

METRIC/IMPERIAL	AMERICAN
15 cloves	15 cloves
4 brown cardamoms, peeled	4 brown cardamoms, peeled
4 (5-cm/2-inch) pieces cinnamon stick	4 (2-inch) pieces cinnamon stick
4 bay leaves	4 bay leaves
8 dry red chillies	8 dry red chilies
20 black peppercorns	20 black peppercorns
1 tablespoon turmeric powder	1 tablespoon turmeric powder
1 tablespoon white cumin seeds	1 tablespoon white cumin seeds
1 tablespoon black cumin seeds	1 tablespoon black cumin seeds
4 tablespoons coriander seeds	$\frac{1}{3}$ cup coriander seeds
$1\frac{1}{2}$ teaspoons fenugreek seeds	$1\frac{1}{2}$ teaspoons fenugreek seeds
$1\frac{1}{2}$ teaspoons mustard seeds	$1\frac{1}{2}$ teaspoons mustard seeds

Roast all the ingredients together in a moderate oven (160°C, 325°F, Gas Mark 3) until they give off an aromatic smell, about 10 minutes. Then grind in an electric grinder or by hand. Press the powder through a sieve. Store in an airtight container – it will last for weeks.

Sambhar musala
Sambhar powder

This powder will come in useful if you are fond of south Indian dishes.

METRIC/IMPERIAL	AMERICAN
50 g/2 oz coriander seeds	6 tablespoons coriander seeds
20 black peppercorns	20 black peppercorns
$\frac{1}{2}$ teaspoon asafoetida powder	$\frac{1}{2}$ teaspoon asafoetida powder
8 curry leaves	8 curry leaves
$1\frac{1}{2}$ teaspoons fenugreek seeds	$1\frac{1}{2}$ teaspoons fenugreek seeds
2 teaspoons white cumin seeds	2 teaspoons white cumin seeds
2 teaspoons turmeric powder	2 teaspoons turmeric powder
2 teaspoons mustard seeds	2 teaspoons mustard seeds
50 g/$\frac{1}{2}$ oz red chillies	$1\frac{1}{2}$ tablespoons red chilies
2 tablespoons mixed dried black beans, chick peas and lentils	3 tablespoons mixed dried black beans, chick peas and lentils

Heat a griddle or heavy-bottomed frying pan and cook each one of the ingredients separately for a few minutes. Grind them all together in an electric grinder or by hand, then press through a sieve. Store in an airtight container.

Dahi
Curd or Indian yogurt

Preparation time 25 minutes
Waiting time 8 hours

*Dahi is an important ingredient in curries, raitas and cool lassis. It is
served as an accompaniment as well as being a marinating and
tenderising agent for chicken and meat.*

METRIC/IMPERIAL
600 ml/1 pint creamy milk
2 tablespoons natural yogurt

AMERICAN
2½ cups creamy milk
3 tablespoons plain yogurt

Bring the milk to the boil in a saucepan then leave to cool for 10 minutes. Beat
the yogurt and add it to the warm milk.

Pour the mixture from one container to another several times to produce a
frothy surface. Pour into a basin, cover and leave overnight in a warm place
or pour into a vacuum flask and leave overnight.

NOTE The colder the weather, the warmer the milk should be when you add
the yogurt, but never add it to very hot milk.

Paneer or Chhena
Indian cream cheese

Preparation time 20 minutes
Waiting time 2 hours
Storage time 2 days

*Home-made cheese of this sort is used in many curries and sweetmeats –
matar paneer is a Punjabi speciality and chhena sweetmeats are very
popular in Bengal.*

METRIC/IMPERIAL
1.15 litres/2 pints Jersey milk
juice of 1 lemon or 2 tablespoons
malt vinegar or 4 tablespoons natural
yogurt

AMERICAN
5 cups Jersey milk
juice of 1 lemon or 3 tablespoons
malt vinegar or ⅓ cup plain yogurt

Bring the milk to the boil in a saucepan. Remove from the heat and stir as the
milk cools to prevent a skin from forming. Add the lemon juice, vinegar or
yogurt and stir until the milk curdles. Pour through a muslin in a sieve, then
draw the corners of the muslin together and, holding tightly, squeeze out the
liquid. Mould the curd mixture in the muslin into a block and press it under a
board for 2 hours. Cut into squares and use as directed in the recipes.

Ghee
Clarified butter

Cooking time 40 minutes
Standing time 2 hours
Storage time 1 year

Ghee is easy to make at home and is the best medium for frying. It can be heated to very high temperatures and therefore is not absorbed into the food, ensuring a crisp result.

METRIC/IMPERIAL	AMERICAN
2.25 kg/5 lb butter	5 lb butter

Melt the butter in a saucepan over a moderate heat and bring to the boil, stirring. Leave the butter to simmer gently for 30 minutes. Remove the pan from the heat and skim the scum from the top using a wooden spatula. Leave the pan to cool for about 2 hours then transfer to a large jar. Discard the salt deposits from the bottom of the pan.

The ghee will weigh about 1.75 kg/4 lb. Store it in a covered container in the refrigerator.

Boondi
Batter drops

Preparation time 15 minutes
Cooking time 20 minutes
Storage time 4 weeks

Keep these boondi in store to make quick sweetmeats and puddings. Although these keep for about a month, it is best not to make too many at a time.

METRIC/IMPERIAL	AMERICAN
225 g/8 oz gram flour	2 cups gram flour
300 ml/$\frac{1}{2}$ pint water	$1\frac{1}{4}$ cups water
oil for deep frying	oil for deep frying

Gradually mix the water into the flour to make a smooth batter. Whisk well and leave for 10 minutes.

Heat the oil in a heavy-bottomed saucepan until a cube of day-old bread turns golden in 1 minute. Using a perforated spoon with round holes, pour the batter into the oil, shaking the spoon so that the batter drops fall through in pieces. Use a little of the batter at a time. Use a clean, perforated spoon to turn the boondi and to take them from the oil. Drain the cooked boondi on absorbent kitchen paper and store in an airtight container for future use.

Chaashni
Syrup

*This basic recipe gives instructions for different strengths of
syrup – use it according to the recipe's requirements.*

METRIC/IMPERIAL
600 ml/1 pint water
2 tablespoons milk
900 g/2 lb sugar

AMERICAN
$2\frac{1}{2}$ cups water
3 tablespoons milk
4 cups sugar

Mix half the water with the milk and divide this mixture into five equal
portions. Dissolve the sugar in the remaining water in a saucepan and bring
to the boil. Now lower the heat to moderate.

After this first boiling, add one of the five reserved portions to the boiling
sugar and stir to mix. Discard any scum from the top. Boil up again and add
the second portion. Discard the scum again and repeat the process with the
next two portions. Use the fifth portion to clean down the sides of the pan. At
this stage the clear syrup is ready for use in most sweetmeats.

The next stage is a one-string syrup. To achieve this, keep boiling the syrup
until a drop of syrup leaves one string between your thumb and finger.
Continue to boil for two, three and four strings. After this stage there will
simply be a lump. This stage is used for sugar candy (misri). With further
boiling you will eventually reach a stage where you can crack the syrup into
chips.

Right *A selection of whole and powdered spices*

1 Ground Ginger
2 Cinnamon Bark
3 Ground Turmeric
4 Paprika
5 Asafoetida
6 Saffron Strands
7 Ground Coriander
8 Black Peppercorns
9 Cinnamon Sticks
10 Cloves
11 Red Chilli Powder
12 Garam Masala
13 Dry Red Chillies
14 Green Mango Powder
15 Ground Cumin
16 Root Ginger

1	6	9	12
2	7	10	13
3			14
4			15
5	8	11	16

1	4	6
2		7
3	5	8
	9	

1 Split Moong Beans

2 Yellow Lentils

3 Skinless Split Black Beans

4 Split Black Beans

5 Moong Beans

6 Chick Peas

7 Red Lentils

8 Split Peas

9 Yellow Moong Beans

Khoya
Dried fresh milk

Preparation time 5 minutes
Cooking time 45 minutes

Apart from the Indian cream cheese, this dried fresh milk is the other common base for Indian sweetmeats and desserts. It is time-consuming to make, but apart from patience and practice, there is nothing to the making of khoya. If you are short of time, buy the ready-made variety.

METRIC/IMPERIAL	AMERICAN
1.15 litres/2 pints milk	5 cups milk
juice of 2 lemons (optional)	juice of 2 lemons (optional)

Bring the milk to the boil in a heavy-bottomed saucepan. Reduce the heat and continue cooking at simmering point. Keep stirring so that the milk does not stick to the base of the pan. As the milk gets thicker, stir more vigorously, using a wooden spoon.

The khoya is cooked when the milk is reduced to a thick, dry lump the consistency of a creamy pastry and it has stopped sizzling.

Remove from the pan and leave to cool. Use within a fortnight.

For a more stylish, granular khoya, add the juice of 2 lemons after the milk has boiled so that the milk coagulates. Then proceed as before. This type of khoya is particularly suitable for burfi.

NOTE Although nothing beats the original, in urgent cases khoya can be made by mixing whole powdered milk (not skimmed) with milk. Add 75 g/3 oz (U.S. 1 cup) dried milk to $1\frac{1}{2}$ tablespoons milk. Cook over a moderate heat as before. Add a little sugar to the milk for sweet khoya.

Previous page *The armoury of the Indian kitchen*
Left *A selection of pulses*

Non-Vegetarian soups

The soup dish is something of a gate-crasher on the traditional Indian gastronomic scene. Indians do not drink soup per se with their meals. Nevertheless, a need for soups arose with the advent of the Raj, when the British Army officers stationed in India required an appetiser before their main meal.

Tale dabalroti ke tukre
Fried bread cubes or croûtons

Serves 8
Preparation time 5 minutes
Cooking time 10 minutes

Fried bread cubes or croûtons add style and texture to the various vegetarian and non-vegetarian soups.

METRIC/IMPERIAL	AMERICAN
4 thick slices bread	4 thick slices bread
oil for deep frying	oil for deep frying

Cut the crusts from the bread and cut the slices into small cubes, as liked. Heat the oil until a cube of day-old bread turns golden in 1 minute. Fry the bread cubes until light brown. Take them out and drain on absorbent kitchen paper. When completely cold, store in an air tight container or a plastic bag. They should easily last a few days without losing their crispness.

Murghi soup
Chicken soup

Serves 4
Preparation time 10 minutes
Cooking time 45 minutes

METRIC/IMPERIAL	AMERICAN
1 tablespoon ghee	1 tablespoon ghee
2 medium onions, chopped	2 medium onions, chopped
900 g/2 lb chicken, cut in pieces	2 lb chicken, cut in pieces
1 litre/1¾ pints water	4¼ cups water
1 teaspoon salt	1 teaspoon salt
½ teaspoon freshly ground black pepper	½ teaspoon freshly ground black pepper
1 teaspoon rice, rinsed	1 teaspoon rice, rinsed
croûtons to serve	croûtons to serve

Heat the ghee in a saucepan and fry the onions until golden brown. Add the chicken and water and bring to the boil. Leave the pan on a low heat for about 30 minutes, until the water reduces and the soup thickens.

Remove the pan from the heat and strain the liquid through a clean cloth. Remove the chicken from the bones and chop the flesh finely. Return it to the soup with the salt, pepper and rice and leave over a low heat for a further 15 minutes. Serve hot with croûtons.

Gosht soup
Meat soup

Serves 4
Preparation time 15 minutes
Cooking time 1¼ hours

This is another popular non-vegetarian soup. There is nothing spectacular about it – it's just a good healthy appetiser. For variety, noodles may be added.

METRIC/IMPERIAL	AMERICAN
450 g/1 lb meat	1 lb meat
900 ml/1½ pints water	3¾ cups water
1 medium onion, chopped	1 medium onion, chopped
1½ teaspoons salt	1½ teaspoons salt
2 cloves garlic, crushed	2 cloves garlic, crushed
1 small piece root ginger (optional)	1 small piece root ginger (optional)
4 small tomatoes, peeled and halved	4 small tomatoes, peeled and halved
50 g/2 oz noodles (optional)	2 oz noodles (optional)
1 tablespoon chopped coriander leaves or mint	1 tablespoon chopped coriander leaves or mint
freshly ground black pepper	freshly ground black pepper

Wash the meat, cut into small pieces and place in a saucepan together with the water, onion, salt, garlic, ginger and tomatoes and bring to the boil. Remove the scum from the surface from time to time, until the soup is clear. Let it simmer over a low heat for about 1 hour, leaving the pan half covered. Then strain the liquid through a sieve, return the meat, add the noodles (if used), coriander or mint and pepper. Return the pan to the heat and simmer for a further 10 minutes, until the noodles are tender. Serve piping hot.

Mansahari mirchi soup
Non-vegetarian mulligatawny soup

Serves 4
Preparation time 10 minutes
Cooking time 1 hour

This dish is the most distinguished preparation from south India known to the West. As its name suggests, it has a large chilli content. You may reduce or increase the proportion of chilli but in any case, mind that skin on your tongue!

METRIC/IMPERIAL	AMERICAN
1 tablespoon ghee	1 tablespoon ghee
1 large onion, chopped	1 large onion, chopped
450 g/1 lb mutton	1 lb mutton
2 teaspoons salt	2 teaspoons salt
2 tablespoons tomato purée	3 tablespoons tomato paste
900 ml/1½ pints meat stock	3¾ cups meat stock
1 large carrot, diced	1 large carrot, diced
1 large cooking apple, peeled, cored and diced	1 large baking apple, peeled, cored and diced
2 lemons, sliced to garnish	2 lemons, sliced to garnish
Paste	*Paste*
4 red chillies	4 red chilies
1 tablespoon coriander seeds	1 tablespoon coriander seeds
1 teaspoon turmeric powder	1 teaspoon turmeric powder
1 teaspoon cumin seeds	1 teaspoon cumin seeds
½ teaspoon grated nutmeg	½ teaspoon grated nutmeg
4 cloves	4 cloves
10 black peppercorns	10 black peppercorns
6 curry leaves	6 curry leaves
2 cloves garlic, crushed	2 cloves garlic, crushed
1 teaspoon grated root ginger	1 teaspoon grated root ginger

First prepare a smooth mixture by grinding all the paste ingredients together. Heat the ghee in a saucepan, add the onion and fry over a moderate heat until the onion is golden. Cut the mutton into small pieces and add to the pan with the paste. Cook for 5 minutes, stirring continuously. Now add the salt, tomato purée and stock and bring to the boil. Lower the heat, cover the pan tightly and leave to simmer for about 30 minutes, or until the meat is tender. Add the carrot and apple and cook for a further 15 minutes.

Remove the pan from the heat and let the soup cool a little. Remove the meat and keep on a plate. With an electric blender, mash the vegetables in the soup or press through a strainer. Return the meat to the strained soup and cook for a further 5 minutes.

Serve hot with slices of lemon.

Palak-haddi soup
Spin-bone soup

Serves 4
Preparation time 10 minutes
Cooking time 40 minutes

This is a good healthful soup which tastes delicious. It is a special favourite of growing children and Popeye fans.

METRIC/IMPERIAL	AMERICAN
900 g/2 lb meaty bones	2 lb meaty bones
900 ml/1½ pints water	3¾ cups water
1 teaspoon salt	1 teaspoon salt
450 g/1 lb spinach, cleaned and chopped	1 lb spinach, cleaned and chopped
2 medium tomatoes, peeled and halved	2 medium tomatoes, peeled and halved
1 medium onion, thickly sliced	1 medium onion, thickly sliced
1 tablespoon cream	1 tablespoon cream
½ teaspoon freshly ground black pepper	½ teaspoon freshly ground black pepper

Wash the bones and boil them with the water and salt over a moderate heat for about 30 minutes. Now add the spinach, tomatoes and onion and leave for a further 10-15 minutes, or until the stock reduces and the soup thickens. Remove the pan from the heat and press the soup through a fine sieve or liquidise without the bones in an electric blender.

Pour a little cream over each serving and sprinkle with pepper.

Gosht
Meat

When meat is referred to in India, it nearly always means goat meat and depending on age of the goat, it is often described as mutton or lamb.
Curries are, of course, the most famous of the Indian meat dishes known in the West, but they are by no means the only dishes the Indian culinary repertoire has to offer!

Preeti kabab
Lovers' nuggets

Serves 6
Preparation time 25 minutes
Cooking time 30 minutes

A loaf of bread, a bottle of chilled wine and a few of these nuggets are all that two lovers need to have their own private party!

METRIC/IMPERIAL	AMERICAN
900 g/2 lb finely minced lean lamb	900 g finely ground lean lamb
1 medium onion, finely chopped	1 medium onion, finely chopped
50 g/2 oz root ginger, grated	2 oz root ginger, grated
8 cloves garlic, crushed	8 cloves garlic, crushed
1 tablespoon coriander seeds, ground	1 tablespoon coriander seeds, ground
4 green chillies, finely chopped	4 green chilies, finely chopped
2½ teaspoons salt	2½ teaspoons salt
2 teaspoons carom seeds	2 teaspoons carom seeds
2 tablespoons chopped coriander leaves	2 tablespoons chopped coriander leaves
pinch of bicarbonate of soda	dash of baking soda
2 egg whites	2 egg whites
6 tablespoons oil	½ cup oil
sauce or chutney to serve	sauce or chutney to serve
Garnish	*Garnish*
2 onions, sliced in rings	2 onions, sliced in rings
4 lemons, sliced	4 lemons, sliced

Mix the first 10 ingredients together thoroughly. Divide the mixture into 18 and mould each portion to a nugget shape.

Whisk the egg white thoroughly and use to coat the nuggets. Heat 1 tablespoon oil at a time in a frying pan and fry the nuggets in batches. Continue to cook over a low heat until they are cooked through.

Serve hot garnished with the onion and lemon with the sauce of your choice.

Seekh kabab
Skewer kababs

Serves 6
Preparation time 1½ hours
Cooking time 30 minutes

These are the most popular type of kababs. They can be deep fried, shallow fried, grilled or roasted on a charcoal fire. What can be more versatile? They taste good any way, but I prefer to roast them directly over a fire. These kababs should always be served hot. Other meats give just as successful results.

METRIC/IMPERIAL
675 g/1½ lb minced mutton
1 teaspoon grated root ginger
1 large onion, finely chopped
25 g/1 oz gram flour
2 green chillies, finely chopped
1 teaspoon green mango powder
1 tablespoon salt
juice of ½ lemon
1 egg
2 tablespoons chopped coriander leaves
50 g/2 oz ghee
slices of tomato, onion and lemon to garnish
Spices
½ teaspoon poppy seeds, roasted and ground
1 teaspoon garam masala
1 tablespoon yellow or red chilli powder
½ teaspoon freshly ground black pepper
1 teaspoon black cumin seeds, roasted and ground
1 tablespoon ground coriander seeds

AMERICAN
1½ lb ground mutton
1 teaspoon grated root ginger
1 large onion, finely chopped
¼ cup gram flour
2 green chilies, finely chopped
1 teaspoon green mango powder
1 tablespoon salt
juice of ½ lemon
1 egg
3 tablespoons chopped coriander leaves
¼ cup ghee
slices of tomato, onion and lemon to garnish
Spices
½ teaspoon poppy seeds, roasted and ground
1 teaspoon garam masala
1 tablespoon yellow or red chili powder
½ teaspoon freshly ground black pepper
1 teaspoon black cumin seeds, roasted and ground
1 tablespoon ground coriander seeds

Mix the mince, ginger, onion, gram flour, chilli, mango powder, salt and lemon juice together with all the spices. Leave for 30 minutes, then mix in the egg and coriander. Knead this mixture until it becomes sticky.

Divide the mixture into 18 portions and form each piece into a sausage shape. Thread the sausages on to skewers – for longer kababs flatten the sausages on the skewers.

Cook under a hot grill or over a charcoal fire, turning frequently. Melt the ghee and brush the kababs all over with it, or use the ghee to fry the kababs.

Serve hot, garnished with the tomato, onion and lemon slices. These are good served with ketchup.

Rogan josh
Mutton curry

Serves 6
Preparation time 20 minutes
Cooking time 2½ hours

This is a dish for which authors and connoisseurs have sung paeans of praises. Its making marked the pinnacle of the culinary craft of Kashmir; the master chefs of the royal Moghul kitchens boasted about perfecting this dish. I take pride in presenting it for you.

METRIC/IMPERIAL
2 tablespoons ghee
675 g/1½ lb mutton
4 bay leaves
1 tablespoon salt
600 ml/1 pint hot water
1 teaspoon garam masala
Spices
2 brown cardamoms
6 cloves
6 black peppercorns
1 teaspoon black cumin seeds
2 (2.5-cm/1-inch) pieces cinnamon stick
Vegetable mixture
2 tablespoons ghee
1 onion, chopped
4 green cardamoms
4 tablespoons tomato purée
1 (142-ml/5-fl oz) carton natural yogurt
Paste
1 onion, chopped
6 cloves garlic
1 tablespoon coriander seeds, roasted
25 g/1 oz root ginger, crushed
1 teaspoon red chilli powder
1½ teaspoons turmeric powder

AMERICAN
3 tablespoons ghee
1½ lb mutton
4 bay leaves
1 tablespoon salt
2½ cups hot water
1 teaspoon garam masala
Spices
2 brown cardamoms
6 cloves
6 black peppercorns
1 teaspoon black cumin seeds
2 (1-inch) pieces cinnamon stick
Vegetable mixture
3 tablespoons ghee
1 onion, chopped
4 green cardamoms
⅓ cup tomato paste
1 (5-fl oz) carton plain yogurt
Paste
1 onion, chopped
6 cloves garlic
1 tablespoon coriander seeds, roasted
1 tablespoon crushed root ginger
1 teaspoon red chili powder
1½ teaspoons turmeric powder

Melt the ghee in a saucepan and cut the meat into 2.5-cm/1-inch cubes. Fry the bay leaf, meat and spices gently for 15 minutes. Transfer to a plate.
 For the vegetable mixture, melt the ghee and fry the onion and cardamoms until golden. Mix in the tomato purée.
 Grind all the paste ingredients together until quite smooth. Mix the paste into the vegetables and cook, stirring continuously, for 5 minutes. Add the yogurt and cook, stirring for a further 5 minutes. Stir in the meat, salt and water. Cover and simmer for 2½ hours, or until the meat is tender. Serve sprinkled with the garam masala.

Bheja rasedaar
Lamb's brains curry

Serves 4
Preparation time 20 minutes
Cooking time 1 hour

This is a dish of good quality but might prove a little costly. It is a rare delight when you can purchase lamb's brains.

METRIC/IMPERIAL	AMERICAN
4 lamb's brains	4 lamb brains
1 teaspoon lemon juice	1 teaspoon lemon juice
300 ml/$\frac{1}{2}$ pint water	1$\frac{1}{4}$ cups water
1 teaspoon salt	1 teaspoon salt
100 g/4 oz ghee	$\frac{1}{2}$ cup ghee
1 large onion, finely chopped	1 large onion, finely chopped
$\frac{1}{4}$ teaspoon garlic powder	$\frac{1}{4}$ teaspoon garlic powder
1 (142-ml/5-fl oz) carton natural yogurt	1 (5-fl oz) carton plain yogurt
2 bay leaves	2 bay leaves
Spices	*Spices*
1 teaspoon ground coriander	1 teaspoon ground coriander
1 teaspoon garam masala	1 teaspoon garam masala
1 teaspoon red chilli powder	1 teaspoon red chili powder
$\frac{1}{2}$ teaspoon ground cinnamon	$\frac{1}{2}$ teaspoon ground cinnamon
4 cloves	4 cloves
1 brown cardamom	1 brown cardamom
6 black peppercorns	6 black peppercorns
Garnish	*Garnish*
225 g/8 oz tomatoes, peeled and halved	$\frac{1}{2}$ lb tomatoes, peeled and halved
4 green cardamoms	4 green cardamoms
1 green chilli, finely chopped	1 green chili, finely chopped

Wash and halve the brains and place in a saucepan with the lemon juice, water and salt. Simmer gently for 15 minutes.

Heat the ghee in another saucepan and fry the onion and garlic powder with the first four spices until golden brown. Fry all together for a few seconds then stir in the yogurt.

Drain the brains, reserving the water, and add them to the onion and spice mixture. Add the remaining spices and the bay leaves and stir thoroughly over a gentle heat until well mixed. Pour in the reserved cooking liquid from the brains, cover and simmer for 20-30 minutes, or until the brains are tender. Transfer to a serving dish.

Arrange the tomatoes over the mixture with the cardamoms and chilli. Leave for 10 minutes before serving.

Nargisi kofte
Nargisi kofta curry

Serves 6
Preparation time 35 minutes
Cooking time 1 hour

METRIC/IMPERIAL	AMERICAN
450 g/1 lb minced mutton	1 lb ground mutton
4 cloves	4 cloves
8 black peppercorns	8 black peppercorns
4 cloves garlic, crushed	4 cloves garlic, crushed
1 green chilli, chopped	1 green chili, chopped
25 g/1 oz root ginger, chopped	1 tablespoon chopped root ginger
pinch of salt	dash of salt
150 ml/$\frac{1}{4}$ pint water	$\frac{2}{3}$ cup water
2 tablespoons chick pea flour	3 tablespoons chick pea flour
1 egg, beaten	1 egg, beaten
6 eggs, hard-boiled	6 eggs, hard-cooked
1 egg white	1 egg white
225 g/8 oz ghee	1 cup ghee
Sauce	*Sauce*
50 g/2 oz ghee	$\frac{1}{4}$ cup ghee
1 large onion, finely chopped	1 large onion, finely chopped
2 bay leaves	2 bay leaves
1 (142-ml/5-fl oz) carton natural yogurt	1 (5-fl oz) carton plain yogurt
salt to taste	salt to taste
2 tablespoons tomato purée	3 tablespoons tomato paste
4 tomatoes, peeled and sliced	4 tomatoes, peeled and sliced
150 ml/$\frac{1}{4}$ pint water	$\frac{2}{3}$ cup water
Spices	*Spices*
1 teaspoon turmeric powder	1 teaspoon turmeric powder
1 teaspoon red chilli powder	1 teaspoon red chili powder
1 teaspoon ground coriander	1 teaspoon ground coriander
1 teaspoon garam masala	1 teaspoon garam masala
chopped parsley or coriander leaves to garnish	chopped parsley or coriander leaves to garnish

Mix the first eight ingredients in a saucepan and simmer for 15 minutes, or until dry. Leave until cool and mix in the chick pea flour and egg. Knead until sticky, divide into six portions and wrap a hard-boiled egg in each. Beat the egg white and brush over the koftas.

Heat the ghee in a frying pan and fry the koftas until golden all over. Drain on absorbent kitchen paper and arrange in a casserole dish.

For the sauce, heat the ghee in a saucepan and fry the onion and bay leaves until light brown. Remove from the heat and stir in all the spices. Return to the heat for about 15 seconds, stirring. Add the yogurt, salt and tomato purée and simmer for 5 minutes, stirring continuously. Mix in the tomato and water. Bring to the boil, stirring. Pour the sauce over the koftas and cook in a moderate oven (180°C, 350°F, Gas Mark 4) for about 15 minutes. Garnish with parsley or coriander.

Yakhini korma
Mutton korma

Serves 4
Preparation time 20 minutes
Cooking time 1½ hours

Mutton in India is not necessarily sheep meat, it is very often goat.
Similarly, kid is often described as lamb. This particular dish is
cooked in the juices from the meat and is scrumptious and wholesome.

METRIC/IMPERIAL	AMERICAN
675 g/1½ lb mutton	1½ lb mutton
600 ml/1 pint water	2½ cups water
100 g/4 oz ghee	½ cup ghee
2 medium onions, finely chopped	2 medium onions, finely chopped
4 bay leaves	4 bay leaves
4 cloves garlic, crushed	4 cloves garlic, crushed
15 g/½ oz root ginger, grated	1 tablespoon grated root ginger
2 (142-ml/5-fl oz) cartons natural yogurt	2 (5-fl oz) cartons plain yogurt
salt to taste	salt to taste
Spices	*Spices*
4 cloves	4 cloves
6 black peppercorns	6 black peppercorns
2 (5-cm/2-inch) pieces cinnamon stick	2 (2-inch) pieces cinnamon stick
1 teaspoon black cumin seeds	1 teaspoon black cumin seeds
2 brown cardamoms	2 brown cardamoms
1 teaspoon turmeric powder	1 teaspoon turmeric powder
1 teaspoon garam masala	1 teaspoon garam masala
1 teaspoon red chilli powder	1 teaspoon red chili powder
Garnish	*Garnish*
1 green chilli, finely chopped	1 green chili, finely chopped
½ teaspoon saffron strands	½ teaspoon saffron strands

Put the first five spices into a small muslin bag. Cut the mutton into 2.5-cm/1-inch cubes and put in a saucepan with the water and muslin bag. Cover and simmer gently until the meat is tender and the water is reduced to half, about 1¼ hours.

In another saucepan melt the ghee and add the onion, bay leaves, garlic and ginger. Fry until the onion is golden, add all the remaining spices and mix well. Cook gently for 5 minutes, stirring continuously. Add the yogurt and salt to taste and cook for a further 5 minutes, stirring. Stir in the cooked meat mixture and juices and discard the muslin bag. Simmer over a low heat for 15 minutes then pour into a heated serving dish.

Scatter the chopped chilli over the top. Steep the saffron in 1 tablespoon hot water and sprinkle over the dish before serving.

Shorwedaar gosht
Lamb curry

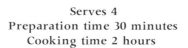

Serves 4
Preparation time 30 minutes
Cooking time 2 hours

This curry could well be made with lamb or kid—either way it is very popular with the meat-eating masses, a very superior concoction. Serve with any rice or bread preparation.

METRIC/IMPERIAL	AMERICAN
675 g/1½ lb lamb	1½ lb lamb
6 tablespoons ghee	½ cup ghee
1 large onion, finely chopped	1 large onion, finely chopped
4 bay leaves	4 bay leaves
2 tablespoons tomato purée	3 tablespoons tomato paste
4 tomatoes, peeled and sliced	4 tomatoes, peeled and sliced
1 (142-ml/5-fl oz) carton natural yogurt	1 (5-fl oz) carton plain yogurt
600 ml/1 pint water	2½ cups water
salt to taste	salt to taste
Spices	*Spices*
6 cloves	6 cloves
6 black peppercorns	6 black peppercorns
1 teaspoon black cumin seeds	1 teaspoon black cumin seeds
2 (2.5-cm/1-inch) pieces cinnamon stick	2 (1-inch) pieces cinnamon stick
1 brown cardamom	1 brown cardamom
2 green cardamoms	2 green cardamoms
1 teaspoon garam masala	1 teaspoon garam masala
Paste	*Paste*
1 medium onion, grated	1 medium onion, grated
6 cloves garlic, crushed	6 cloves garlic, crushed
1 (2.5-cm/1-inch) piece root ginger, chopped	1 (1-inch) piece root ginger, chopped
1 tablespoon coriander seeds	1 tablespoon coriander seeds
1 teaspoon red chilli powder	1 teaspoon red chili powder
1 teaspoon turmeric powder	1 teaspoon turmeric powder
½ teaspoon ground cinnamon	½ teaspoon ground cinnamon

Cut the lamb into 2.5-cm/1-inch cubes. Heat one-third of the ghee in a saucepan and fry the lamb with the first five spices for 10 minutes, stirring continuously. Transfer to a dish and keep hot.

Heat the remaining ghee and fry the onion, bay leaves and green cardamoms until golden brown. Grind all the paste ingredients together to a fairly smooth consistency. Add this to the onion mixture and fry, stirring, for 30 seconds. Add the tomato purée, tomato and yogurt and cook for 10 minutes. Stir in the meat mixture and simmer gently for 5-6 minutes. Pour in the water, add salt to taste and simmer until the meat is tender, about 1½ hours. Sprinkle the garam masala over the curry just before serving.

Suwar ka gosht
Pork

Contrary to the impression held in the West, pork is eaten and well liked by a large section of the meat-eating population. Pork is not always obtained from wild roaming pigs, either; I know of several establishments where large sums of money are spent on pig farming.

Shikar korma
Pork korma

Serves 4
Preparation time 15 minutes
Cooking time 2 hours

METRIC/IMPERIAL	AMERICAN
450 g/1 lb pork	1 lb pork
150 g/5 oz ghee	$\frac{2}{3}$ cup ghee
1 (142-ml/5-fl oz) carton natural yogurt	1 (5-fl oz) carton plain yogurt
1½ teaspoons salt	1½ teaspoons salt
juice of ½ lemon	juice of ½ lemon
1 large onion, coarsely chopped	1 large onion, coarsely chopped
4 cloves garlic, crushed	4 cloves garlic, crushed
4 bay leaves	4 bay leaves
300 ml/½ pint water	1¼ cups water
Spices	*Spices*
1 teaspoon garam masala	1 teaspoon garam masala
4 cloves	4 cloves
1 brown cardamom	1 brown cardamom
1 teaspoon red chilli powder	1 teaspoon red chili powder
1 teaspoon turmeric powder	1 teaspoon turmeric powder

Cut the pork into 2.5-cm/1-inch cubes. Heat 25 g/1 oz (U.S. 2 tablespoons) of the ghee in a saucepan and fry the pork for 10-15 minutes over a low heat. Add the garam masala, yogurt, salt and lemon juice and cook, stirring, for 2 minutes. Remove and stand for 2 hours.

Heat the remaining ghee and fry the onion and garlic until golden. Set aside, then, in the remaining ghee, quickly fry the bay leaves and the remaining spices. Stir in the pork, onion and water and simmer, covered, until the pork is tender, about 1½ hours.

Pasinda tikka
Boneless pork croquettes

Serves 6
Preparation time 4½ hours
Cooking time 30 minutes

This dish comes to you from the Punjab with love. These tikkas taste superlative when barbecued, but even when they are grilled, they taste nothing short of first class. They can be served as a tea time snack or as a side dish with a main meal. I suspect they would go down particularly well with drinks.

METRIC/IMPERIAL	AMERICAN
675 g/1½ lb pork	1½ lb pork
1 (142-ml/5-fl oz) carton natural yogurt	1 (5-fl oz) carton plain yogurt
½ tablespoon vinegar	½ tablespoon vinegar
2 teaspoons salt	2 teaspoons salt
2 tablespoons ghee	3 tablespoons ghee
2 medium onions, sliced in rings	2 medium onions, sliced in rings
6 lemons, sliced	6 lemons, sliced
sauce or chutney to serve	sauce or chutney to serve
Paste	*Paste*
4 red chillies	4 red chilies
10 cloves garlic, crushed	10 cloves garlic, crushed
2 teaspoons garam masala	2 teaspoons garam masala
2 teaspoons grated root ginger	2 teaspoons grated root ginger

First prepare a smooth mixture by grinding all the paste ingredients together.

Beat the pork with a meat pounder and cut it into 2.5-cm/1-inch cubes. Place the cubes on a wooden board and prick them with a fork. Mix the yogurt, vinegar, salt and paste together and rub all over the pork. Leave to marinate for 4 hours.

Thread the meat on skewers and cook under a hot grill until tender. Keep turning them over so that they are well cooked on all sides. When the tikkas are cooked, remove them from the skewers and shallow fry them in a little ghee.

Serve hot, with the onion rings, slices of lemon and the sauce or chutney of your choosing.

Suwar ka gosht aur palak
Pork and spinach

Serves 4
Preparation time 15 minutes
Cooking time 2 hours

Spinach adds variety to this popular dish — eat it with a bread or rice preparation.

METRIC/IMPERIAL	AMERICAN
450 g/1 lb pork	1 lb pork
175 g/6 oz ghee	$\frac{3}{4}$ cup ghee
1 large onion, chopped	1 large onion, chopped
6 cloves garlic, crushed	6 cloves garlic, crushed
4 bay leaves	4 bay leaves
225 g/8 oz tomatoes, peeled and sliced	$\frac{1}{2}$ lb tomatoes, peeled and sliced
225 g/8 oz spinach, chopped	$\frac{1}{2}$ lb spinach, chopped
salt to taste	salt to taste
25 g/1 oz root ginger, grated	2 tablespoons grated root ginger
300 ml/$\frac{1}{2}$ pint water	$1\frac{1}{4}$ cups water
50 g/2 oz butter	$\frac{1}{4}$ cup butter
Spices	*Spices*
1 teaspoon white cumin seeds	1 teaspoon white cumin seeds
1 teaspoon turmeric powder	1 teaspoon turmeric powder
1 teaspoon red chilli powder	1 teaspoon red chili powder
1 tablespoon garam masala	1 tablespoon garam masala

Cut the pork into 2.5-cm/1-inch cubes. Heat the ghee in a saucepan and fry the onion, garlic, bay leaves and cumin seeds until the onion is golden brown. Add the meat with the turmeric and chilli powders. Stir well then add the tomato and spinach. Add salt to taste with the ginger and garam masala. Cover and leave over a low heat for 15 minutes. Stir over a low heat for 5 minutes, until the ghee starts to separate.

Add the water and simmer gently until the pork is tender, about $1\frac{1}{2}$ hours. This dish should be moist, but without too much gravy. Melt the butter and pour it over the dish just before serving.

Gaay ka gosht
Beef

Beef is taboo for the Hindus as pork is for the Muslims. They believe the cow is sacred, so they will not touch her.

Gaay gosht keema
Minced beef curry

Serves 4
Preparation time 15 minutes
Cooking time 1½ hours

This is a basic minced meat dish; mutton or pork can be substituted for beef. Eat with paraunthas or rice.

METRIC/IMPERIAL	AMERICAN
100 g/4 oz ghee	½ cup ghee
1 large onion, finely chopped	1 large onion, finely chopped
4 cloves garlic, crushed	4 cloves garlic, crushed
2 bay leaves	2 bay leaves
15 g/½ oz root ginger, grated	1 tablespoon grated root ginger
2 tablespoons natural yogurt	3 tablespoons plain yogurt
2 tablespoons tomato purée	3 tablespoons tomato paste
450 g/1 lb minced beef	1 lb ground beef
300 ml/½ pint water	1¼ cups water
salt to taste	salt to taste
chopped parsley or coriander leaves	chopped parsley or coriander leaves
to garnish	to garnish
Spices	*Spices*
4 cloves	4 cloves
4 green cardamoms, crushed	4 green cardamoms, crushed
½ teaspoon garam masala	½ teaspoon garam masala
1 teaspoon turmeric powder	1 teaspoon turmeric powder
½ teaspoon ground cinnamon	½ teaspoon ground cinnamon
½ teaspoon red chilli powder	½ teaspoon red chili powder

Heat the ghee in a frying pan and fry the onion, garlic, bay leaves and cloves until the onion is golden brown. Remove from the heat and add the ginger, yogurt, tomato purée and all the remaining spices. Fry for about 5 minutes, stirring occasionally.

Add the mince to the pan and fry, stirring continuously, for 5 minutes. Add the water and salt and mix well. Cover and leave to simmer gently for 1 hour. This dish should be moist, but without excess gravy. Serve hot, garnished with the parsley or coriander.

Right *Preparation for Beef korma (see page 50).*

Kanpuri kofte
Beef kofta curry

Serves 4
Preparation time 30 minutes
Cooking time 45 minutes

METRIC/IMPERIAL	AMERICAN
450 g/1 lb minced beef	1 lb ground beef
1 tablespoon coconut flour	1 tablespoon coconut flour
1 egg	1 egg
100 g/4 oz ghee	$\frac{1}{2}$ cup ghee
1 large onion, finely chopped	1 large onion, finely chopped
2 cloves garlic, crushed	2 cloves garlic, crushed
2 bay leaves	2 bay leaves
2 tablespoons natural yogurt	3 tablespoons plain yogurt
2 tablespoons tomato purée	3 tablespoons tomato paste
salt to taste	salt to taste
300 ml/$\frac{1}{2}$ pint water	1$\frac{1}{4}$ cups water
chopped parsley or coriander leaves	chopped parsley or coriander leaves
to garnish	to garnish
Spices	*Spices*
$\frac{1}{2}$ teaspoon garam masala	$\frac{1}{2}$ teaspoon garam masala
$\frac{1}{2}$ teaspoon ground cinnamon	$\frac{1}{2}$ teaspoon ground cinnamon
$\frac{1}{2}$ teaspoon ground ginger	$\frac{1}{2}$ teaspoon ground ginger
4 green cardamoms	4 green cardamoms
4 cloves	4 cloves
1 teaspoon turmeric powder	1 teaspoon turmeric powder
1 teaspoon red chilli powder	1 teaspoon red chili powder
$\frac{1}{2}$ teaspoon ground ginger	$\frac{1}{2}$ teaspoon ground ginger
$\frac{1}{2}$ teaspoon garam masala	$\frac{1}{2}$ teaspoon garam masala

Mix the mince with the coconut flour, egg, garam masala, cinnamon and ginger. Roll the mixture into plum-sized balls and set aside.

Heat the ghee in a saucepan and add the onion, garlic, bay leaves, cardamoms and cloves. Fry until golden brown. Remove from the heat and stir in the yogurt, tomato purée, salt and all the remaining spices. Return to the heat and cook for 5 minutes, stirring occasionally. Pour in the water and add the meatballs to the pan and bring to the boil. Cover and cook over a low heat for 30 minutes. Serve hot, garnished with parsley or coriander.

Previous page *Pea and cream cheese pullao (see page 111); Beef korma (see page 50); Fried okra (see page 99).*
Left *Leavened baked bread (see page 133); Grilled chicken (see page 54).*

Shahi korma
Beef korma

Serves 4
Preparation time 1½ hours
Cooking time 1 hour

As with all other beef recipes, another meat can be substituted for beef. This is a rich and rather classy dish—serve it with pullaos.

METRIC/IMPERIAL	AMERICAN
1 large onion, chopped	1 large onion, chopped
25 g/1 oz blanched almonds	¼ cup blanched almonds
15 g/½ oz root ginger, chopped	1 tablespoon chopped root ginger
salt to taste	salt to taste
450 g/1 lb chuck steak	1 lb chuck steak
225 g/8 oz ghee	1 cup ghee
1 large onion, finely chopped	1 large onion, finely chopped
4 bay leaves	4 bay leaves
1 (142-ml/5-fl oz) carton natural yogurt	1 (5-fl oz) carton plain yogurt
150 ml/¼ pint single cream	⅔ cup light cream
150 ml/¼ pint water	⅔ cup water
Spices	*Spices*
1 tablespoon roasted coriander seeds	1 tablespoon roasted coriander seeds
1 teaspoon black cumin seeds	1 teaspoon black cumin seeds
4 cloves	4 cloves
1 brown cardamom	1 brown cardamom
4 black peppercorns	4 black peppercorns
4 green cardamoms	4 green cardamoms
1 teaspoon red chilli powder	1 teaspoon red chili powder
1 teaspoon turmeric powder	1 teaspoon turmeric powder
½ teaspoon saffron strands	½ teaspoon saffron strands
1 teaspoon garam masala	1 teaspoon garam masala

Mix together the onion, almonds, ginger, salt and the first five spices and grind to a smooth paste. Cut the beef into 2.5-cm/1-inch cubes and coat liberally with the prepared paste. Set aside for 2 hours.

Heat the ghee in a saucepan and fry the onion and bay leaves until golden. Take half the fried onion and set aside. Add the yogurt, green cardamoms and chilli and turmeric powders to the remaining onion and continue frying until the liquid has dried up. Add the coated meat and stir well.

Beat the cream with the saffron and add to the meat mixture with the garam masala and reserved fried onions. Add the water and simmer, covered, for 1 hour, or until the meat is tender.

Gaay gosht do-piazza
Beef with onions

Serves 4
Preparation time 20 minutes
Cooking time 2 hours

Mutton or lamb may be used instead of beef. The main feature of this dish is the preponderance of onions. Muslims love this dish – according to an old Hindu saying, a newly converted Muslim eats a lot of onions! The dish should be moist but without too much liquid.

METRIC/IMPERIAL	AMERICAN
4 large onions	4 large onions
100 g/4 oz ghee	$\frac{1}{2}$ cup ghee
2 bay leaves	2 bay leaves
450 g/1 lb beef	1 lb beef
4 cloves garlic, crushed	4 cloves garlic, crushed
2 (142-ml/5-fl oz) cartons natural yogurt	2 (5-fl oz) cartons plain yogurt
300 ml/$\frac{1}{2}$ pint water	1$\frac{1}{4}$ cups water
salt to taste	salt to taste
Spices	*Spices*
1 teaspoon ground ginger	1 teaspoon ground ginger
1 teaspoon black cumin seeds	1 teaspoon black cumin seeds
4 cloves	4 cloves
6 black peppercorns	6 black peppercorns
1 brown cardamom	1 brown cardamom
4 green cardamoms	4 green cardamoms
$\frac{1}{2}$ teaspoon ground cinnamon	$\frac{1}{2}$ teaspoon ground cinnamon
1 teaspoon red chilli powder	1 teaspoon red chilli powder
Topping	*Topping*
1 teaspoon garam masala	1 teaspoon garam masala
6 tomatoes, peeled and halved	6 tomatoes, peeled and halved
chopped parsley or coriander leaves	chopped parsley or coriander leaves

Finely chop one onion and thickly slice the rest. Heat the ghee in a flameproof casserole and fry the chopped onion with the ginger until golden. Drain well and transfer to a plate. Add the cumin, cloves, peppercorns, brown and green cardamoms and bay leaves to the pan and stir well.

Cut the meat into pieces and add to the spices in the pan with the sliced onion and garlic. Mix well and stir in the cinnamon, chilli and yogurt. Cook gently over a low heat for 15 minutes. Pour in the water and salt and mix well. Cover and cook for 1$\frac{1}{2}$ hours, or until the meat is tender. Cover the dish with the garam masala, tomatoes and parsley or coriander and cook in a moderate oven (180°C, 350°F, Gas Mark 4) for 10 minutes.

Batakh
Duck

Duck is rich and juicy and is often used in Indian dishes. The meat is rather greasy, so when substituting duck for other meat, reduce the quantity of cooking oil.

Batakh rasedaar
Duck curry

Serves 6
Preparation time 1¼ hours
Cooking time 1¾ hours

This is a rich and juicy dish, full of natural oils and a great favourite with connoisseurs.

METRIC/IMPERIAL	AMERICAN
1 tablespoon lime juice	1 tablespoon lime juice
½–1 tablespoon salt	½–1 tablespoon salt
675 g/1½ lb duck portions	1½ lb duck portions
100 g/4 oz ghee	½ cup ghee
2 large onions, finely chopped	2 large onions, finely chopped
1 teaspoon turmeric powder	1 teaspoon turmeric powder
1 teaspoon red chilli powder	1 teaspoon red chili powder
2 tablespoons natural yogurt	3 tablespoons plain yogurt
2 cloves garlic, crushed	2 cloves garlic, crushed
15 g/½ oz root ginger, chopped	1 tablespoon chopped root ginger
300 ml/½ pint water	1¼ cups water
6 tomatoes, peeled and halved	6 tomatoes, peeled and halved
Garnish	*Garnish*
1 teaspoon garam masala	1 teaspoon garam masala
chopped coriander leaves	chopped coriander leaves

Mix the lime juice and salt, rub over the duck and leave for 1 hour.

Heat the ghee in a flameproof casserole and fry half the onion until golden brown. Add the turmeric and chilli powders and yogurt. Stir for 2 minutes over a moderate heat. Make a paste by grinding together the remaining onion, garlic and ginger. Add this to the mixture and cook, stirring, until the ghee starts to separate. Stir in the water and bring to the boil. Add the duck, cover and simmer for 1½ hours.

Cover with the tomatoes and cook in a moderate oven (180°C, 350°F, Gas Mark 4) for 10 minutes. Garnish with garam masala and coriander.

Murghi
Chicken

Poultry is a bit on the expensive side in India and therefore the common man cooks it only on special occasions. The royalty, the Nawabs and the patricians of India do not tire of eating chicken delicacies. Tandoori murgha, murgha musallam and grilled drumsticks are but a few of the virtually infinite possibilities.

Tandoori murgha taangen
Grilled drumsticks

Serves 4
Preparation time 25 minutes
Cooking time 30 minutes

This succulent savoury dish can be eaten as a snack or a side dish. However, it requires constant attention for perfect results.

METRIC/IMPERIAL	AMERICAN
900 g/2 lb chicken drumsticks	2 lb chicken drumsticks
2 teaspoons salt	2 teaspoons salt
4 tablespoons special tandoori chicken powder	$\frac{1}{3}$ cup special tandoori chicken powder
4 tablespoons oil	$\frac{1}{3}$ cup oil
2 tablespoons lemon juice	3 tablespoons lemon juice
2 medium onions, sliced	2 medium onions, sliced
4 lemons, sliced in rounds	4 lemons, sliced in rounds

Remove the skin from the drumsticks and place them on a baking sheet. Now mix the salt and tandoori powder and rub half of it on one side of the drumsticks. Then turn them over and use the other half on the other side. Prick the meat on the drumsticks using a fork.

Pour half of the oil over the drumsticks and put the baking sheet under the grill at a low heat. When the drumsticks get slightly brown, take them out, turn them over and pour the rest of the oil over them. Return to the grill once again. When both sides are browned, continue until the chicken is cooked (test with a fork). Pour the lemon juice over the drumsticks.

Fry the onions in some of the remaining oil. Serve hot on a bed of fried onion rings and slices of lemon.

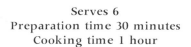

Tandoori murgha
Baked chicken

Serves 6
Preparation time 30 minutes
Cooking time 1 hour

Tandoori cooking is the culmination of the Indian culinary art. It was originally a Punjabi way of cooking food, now adopted and prevalent worldwide. Tandoori chicken is one of the most famous of all Indian dishes. It is economical and easy to make and has a taste and deliciousness which defy description. An excellent dish which can be served with one of the Indian breads such as a naan or with a rice pullao.

METRIC/IMPERIAL	AMERICAN
1.5 kg/3 lb chicken	3 lb chicken
2 teaspoons salt	2 teaspoons salt
2 tablespoons lemon juice	3 tablespoons lemon juice
4 tablespoons ghee	$\frac{1}{3}$ cup ghee
$\frac{1}{2}$ teaspoon saffron strands	$\frac{1}{2}$ teaspoon saffron strands
Paste	*Paste*
4 red chillies	4 red chilies
$1\frac{1}{2}$ teaspoons turmeric powder	$1\frac{1}{2}$ teaspoons turmeric powder
2 tablespoons coriander seeds	3 tablespoons coriander seeds
2 teaspoons garam masala	2 teaspoons garam masala
6 cloves garlic, crushed	6 cloves garlic, crushed
1 medium onion, coarsely chopped	1 medium onion, coarsely chopped
15 g/$\frac{1}{2}$ oz root ginger, grated	1 tablespoon grated root ginger
Garnish	*Garnish*
4 lemons, sliced in rounds	4 lemons, sliced in rounds
1 medium onion, sliced in rings	1 medium onion, sliced in rings

First make a smooth mixture by grinding all the paste ingredients together. Remove the skin from the chicken and steam cook it over water for about 10 minutes. Drain off the water, place the chicken on a platter, then prick it all over with a fork. Mix the salt and lemon juice into the paste and rub it all over the chicken and also inside it. Leave it to permeate the flesh for about 10 minutes.

Warm the ghee in a large saucepan over a low heat. Sprinkle the saffron over it and then carefully lower the chicken into the pan. Cook turning it over occasionally for about 10 minutes. Then transfer the contents to a casserole with a lid, and leave it in a moderately hot oven (200°C, 400°F, Gas Mark 6) for 30 minutes, or until the chicken is tender.

Serve hot with slices of lemon and onion rings.

Murgha korma
Chicken korma

Serves 4
Preparation time 20 minutes
Cooking time 50 minutes

This is a recipe for a genuine korma, as cooked in the Nawabs' courts.
For variety add ½ teaspoon saffron strands just before serving,
or add cashew nuts or almonds with the tomatoes.

METRIC/IMPERIAL	AMERICAN
175 g/6 oz ghee	¾ cup ghee
2 medium onions, finely chopped	2 medium onions, finely chopped
6 cloves garlic, crushed	6 cloves garlic, crushed
4 tablespoons natural yogurt	⅓ cup plain yogurt
2 bay leaves	2 bay leaves
salt to taste	salt to taste
4 chicken portions	4 chicken portions
225 g/8 oz tomatoes, peeled and sliced	½ lb tomatoes, peeled and sliced
1 tablespoon lemon juice	1 tablespoon lemon juice
450 ml/¾ pint water	2 cups water
Spices	*Spices*
4 cloves	4 cloves
8 black peppercorns	8 black peppercorns
2 (2.5-cm/1-inch) pieces cinnamon stick	2 (1-inch) pieces cinnamon stick
1 teaspoon brown cardamom seeds	1 teaspoon brown cardamom seeds
1 teaspoon black cumin seeds	1 teaspoon black cumin seeds
1 teaspoon ground ginger	1 teaspoon ground ginger
1 teaspoon red chilli powder	1 teaspoon red chili powder
1 teaspoon garam masala	1 teaspoon garam masala

Heat the ghee in a saucepan and fry the onion until golden brown. Set aside half the cooked onion. Add the first seven spices to the onion left in the pan, along with the garlic, yogurt, bay leaves and salt. Stir over a low heat for 5 minutes.

Add the chicken portions to the pan and cook gently for 5 minutes. Stir in the tomatoes, lemon juice and garam masala and stir well.

Stirring continuously, pour in the water, cover and simmer for 30-40 minutes, or until the chicken is tender.

Murghi vindaloo
Chicken vindaloo

Serves 6
Preparation time 1½ hours
Cooking time 45 minutes

Vindaloo is a delicacy brought to perfection by the southern Indians and also the Goanese. It is usually made very hot and sour. It is the hottest curry of south India where even the mild curries are hotter than the hot curries elsewhere. One thing should be noted here; the reduction in the amount of chillies will not alter the basic structure of this dish, as 'vindaloo' is a method of making this variety of dishes, and not the name of a dish.

METRIC/IMPERIAL	AMERICAN
900 g/2 lb chicken, cut in pieces	2 lb chicken, cut in pieces
6 tablespoons mustard oil	½ cup mustard oil
4 bay leaves	4 bay leaves
1 large onion, thinly sliced	1 large onion, thinly sliced
1 teaspoon salt	1 teaspoon salt
10 cloves garlic, crushed	10 cloves garlic, crushed
15 g/½ oz root ginger, thinly sliced	1 tablespoon thinly sliced root ginger
2 medium tomatoes, peeled and quartered	2 medium tomatoes, peeled and quartered
150 ml/¼ pint tamarind juice	⅔ cup tamarind juice
300 ml/½ pint water	1¼ cups water
2 teaspoons desiccated coconut to garnish	2 teaspoons shredded coconut to garnish
Spices	*Spices*
1 teaspoon green cardamom seeds	1 teaspoon green cardamom seeds
2 teaspoons turmeric powder	2 teaspoons turmeric powder
1 teaspoon paprika	1 teaspoon paprika pepper
Paste	*Paste*
2 tablespoons vindaloo powder	3 tablespoons vindaloo powder
2 teaspoons vinegar	2 teaspoons vinegar
2 teaspoons salt	2 teaspoons salt

First combine the paste ingredients to make a smooth mixture. Make a few deep gashes on the chicken pieces and rub the paste over them. Leave to marinate for 1 hour.

Heat the mustard oil in a saucepan over a moderate heat. Add the bay leaves and cardamom seeds, stir, then add the onion and fry until light brown. Then add the remaining spices, stir well and add the chicken pieces. Continue to cook, stirring, for about 5 minutes. Add the salt, garlic, ginger and tomatoes and cook for a further 10 minutes, still stirring.

When the fat starts separating, add the tamarind juice together with the water. Stir once or twice. Cover with a tightly fitting lid, lower the heat and leave to simmer for about 25 minutes until the chicken is tender.

Garnish with the desiccated coconut and serve hot.

Murghi do-piazza
Chicken with onions

Serves 4
Preparation time 40 minutes
Cooking time 1¼ hours

This dish pleases those who like a preponderance of onions – adapt the quantity of onions to your liking.

METRIC/IMPERIAL	AMERICAN
1 chicken	1 chicken
½-1 tablespoon salt	½-1 tablespoon salt
2 tablespoons lemon juice	3 tablespoons lemon juice
175 g/6 oz ghee	¾ cup ghee
4 large onions, coarsely chopped	4 large onions, coarsely chopped
2 cloves garlic, crushed	2 cloves garlic, crushed
2 (142-ml/5-fl oz) cartons natural yogurt	2 (5-fl oz) cartons plain yogurt
300 ml/½ pint water	1¼ cups water
Spices	*Spices*
6 cloves	6 cloves
1 brown cardamom	1 brown cardamom
12 black peppercorns	12 black peppercorns
2 (2.5-cm/1-inch) pieces cinnamon stick	2 (1-inch) pieces cinnamon stick
½ teaspoon ground ginger	½ teaspoon ground ginger
1 teaspoon turmeric powder	1 teaspoon turmeric powder
1 teaspoon red chilli powder	1 teaspoon red chili powder
Topping	*Topping*
1 teaspoon garam masala	1 teaspoon garam masala
225 g/8 oz tomatoes, peeled and halved	½ lb tomatoes, peeled and halved
1 medium onion, chopped and fried	1 medium onion, chopped and fried

Cut the chicken into four or eight pieces. Mix the salt and lemon juice and rub all over the chicken. Set aside for 30 minutes.

Heat the ghee in a flameproof casserole and add the first four spices. Stir well then add the chicken, onion, garlic and remaining spices. Cook gently for 15 minutes, stirring continuously.

Add the yogurt and stir for 5 minutes over a low heat. Add the water, cover and simmer for 40-50 minutes, or until the chicken is tender.

Sprinkle the top with garam masala, arrange the tomatoes around the dish and cover with the onion. Cook in a moderate oven (180°C, 350°F, Gas Mark 4) for 10 minutes before serving.

Murgha musallam
Whole chicken

Serves 6
Preparation time 2½ hours
Cooking time 1½ hours

<table>
<tr><td align="center">METRIC/IMPERIAL</td><td align="center">AMERICAN</td></tr>
<tr><td align="center">10 cloves garlic, crushed</td><td align="center">10 cloves garlic, crushed</td></tr>
<tr><td align="center">25 g/1 oz root ginger, grated</td><td align="center">2 tablespoons grated root ginger</td></tr>
<tr><td align="center">salt as specified</td><td align="center">salt as specified</td></tr>
<tr><td align="center">1 (142-ml/5-fl oz) carton natural
yogurt</td><td align="center">1 (5-fl oz) carton plain yogurt</td></tr>
<tr><td align="center">1 tablespoon lemon juice</td><td align="center">1 tablespoon lemon juice</td></tr>
<tr><td align="center">1 chicken</td><td align="center">1 chicken</td></tr>
<tr><td align="center">225 g/8 oz long-grain rice</td><td align="center">1 cup long-grain rice</td></tr>
<tr><td align="center">100 g/4 oz shelled peas</td><td align="center">¾ cup shelled peas</td></tr>
<tr><td align="center">6 bay leaves</td><td align="center">6 bay leaves</td></tr>
<tr><td align="center">225 g/8 oz ghee</td><td align="center">1 cup ghee</td></tr>
<tr><td align="center">2 large onions, finely chopped</td><td align="center">2 large onions, finely chopped</td></tr>
<tr><td align="center">225 g/8 oz tomatoes, peeled and sliced</td><td align="center">½ lb tomatoes, peeled and sliced</td></tr>
<tr><td align="center">450 ml/¾ pint hot water</td><td align="center">2 cups hot water</td></tr>
<tr><td align="center">2 tablespoons chopped parsley or
coriander leaves</td><td align="center">3 tablespoons chopped parsley or
coriander leaves</td></tr>
<tr><td align="center">Spices</td><td align="center">Spices</td></tr>
<tr><td align="center">2 teaspoons garam masala</td><td align="center">2 teaspoons garam masala</td></tr>
<tr><td align="center">1 tablespoon turmeric powder</td><td align="center">1 tablespoon turmeric powder</td></tr>
<tr><td align="center">8 cloves</td><td align="center">8 cloves</td></tr>
<tr><td align="center">6 black peppercorns</td><td align="center">6 black peppercorns</td></tr>
<tr><td align="center">1 brown cardamom</td><td align="center">1 brown cardamom</td></tr>
<tr><td align="center">4 green cardamoms, crushed</td><td align="center">4 green cardamoms, crushed</td></tr>
<tr><td align="center">1 teaspoon red chilli powder</td><td align="center">1 teaspoon red chili powder</td></tr>
<tr><td align="center">1 tablespoon roasted coriander</td><td align="center">1 tablespoon roasted coriander</td></tr>
<tr><td align="center">1 teaspoon black cumin seeds</td><td align="center">1 teaspoon black cumin seeds</td></tr>
<tr><td align="center">½ teaspoon saffron strands</td><td align="center">½ teaspoon saffron strands</td></tr>
</table>

Mix three-quarters of the garlic with half the ginger, half the garam masala, 1 tablespoon salt, one-third of the turmeric, half the yogurt and the lemon juice and mix to a paste. Make small cuts in the chicken flesh and rub the paste all over and in the cavity. Leave for 2 hours.

Half cook the rice with the peas, the remaining garlic, 4 cloves, peppercorns, ½ teaspoon salt, brown cardamom and 4 bay leaves and water and use to stuff the chicken.

Heat half the ghee in a saucepan and fry the chicken until brown all over, being careful not to let the stuffing out. Drain the chicken.

In a flameproof casserole, fry half the onion in the remaining ghee with 2 bay leaves, remaining cloves and green cardamoms, until golden. Add the remaining turmeric and the chilli powder. Make a paste by grinding together the coriander and cumin seeds and the remaining onion and grated ginger. Cook, stirring, for 5-10 minutes, until the ghee starts to separate. Add the remaining yogurt, the tomato and ½ teaspoon salt.

Add the chicken to the pan and baste with the spice mixture. Pour over 300 ml/½ pint (U.S. 1¼ cups) water, cover and cook in a moderately hot oven (200°C, 400°F, Gas Mark 6) for 1 hour.

Steep the saffron in the remaining water and sprinkle over the chicken 10 minutes before the end of the cooking time. Sprinkle with the remaining garam masala and coriander or parsley before serving.

Rasedaar murghi taangen
Chicken curry

Serves 4
Preparation time 15 minutes
Cooking time 50 minutes

METRIC/IMPERIAL	AMERICAN
100 g/4 oz ghee	½ cup ghee
2 medium onions, finely chopped	2 medium onions, finely chopped
4 cloves garlic, crushed	4 cloves garlic, crushed
2 tablespoons tomato purée	3 tablespoons tomato paste
15 g/½ oz root ginger, chopped	1 tablespoon chopped root ginger
1 tablespoon lemon juice	1 tablespoon lemon juice
8 chicken drumsticks	8 chicken drumsticks
4 tablespoons natural yogurt	⅓ cup plain yogurt
300 ml/½ pint hot water	1¼ cups hot water
salt to taste	salt to taste
Spices	*Spices*
4 cloves	4 cloves
1 (5-cm/2-inch) piece cinnamon stick	1 (2-inch) piece cinnamon stick
4 black peppercorns	4 black peppercorns
1 brown cardamom	1 brown cardamom
2 green cardamoms	2 green cardamoms
1 teaspoon turmeric powder	1 teaspoon turmeric powder
1 teaspoon red chilli powder	1 teaspoon red chili powder
Garnish	*Garnish*
1 teaspoon garam masala	1 teaspoon garam masala
1 tablespoon chopped parsley or coriander leaves	1 tablespoon chopped parsley or coriander leaves

Heat the ghee in a saucepan and fry the onion, garlic and the first five spices until golden brown.

Add the tomato purée, ginger, lemon juice, chicken drumsticks, and turmeric and chilli powders. Mix well and cook for 15 minutes over a low heat.

Mix together the yogurt, hot water and salt and stir into the chicken mixture. Bring to the boil then cover and simmer for about 30 minutes or until the chicken is tender. Sprinkle with garam masala and parsley or coriander before serving.

Machhli
Fish

There are plenty of piscatorial delights in the crowded corridors of the Indian cuisine. India has a coast line stretching for over 2,500 miles and these and internal waters supply over 2,000 varieties of fish. The Riparian population thrive on fish. They cook it by steaming, baking, roasting, grilling, poaching, frying and currying. Fish is rich in protein, calcium and Vitamin D. These dishes are quick and easy to make.

Bharwan machhli
Stuffed herrings

Serves 4
Preparation time 20 minutes
Cooking time 20 minutes

Serve as a side dish with a non-vegetarian meal for a special occasion.

METRIC/IMPERIAL	AMERICAN
50 g/2 oz butter	$\frac{1}{4}$ cup butter
1 large onion, chopped	1 large onion, chopped
1 teaspoon white cumin seeds	1 teaspoon white cumin seeds
1 teaspoon grated root ginger	1 teaspoon grated root ginger
salt to taste	salt to taste
2 green chillies, finely chopped	2 green chilies, finely chopped
1 tablespoon chopped coriander leaves	1 tablespoon chopped coriander leaves
1 tablespoon lemon juice	1 tablespoon lemon juice
450 g/1 lb potatoes, peeled, boiled and crushed	$\frac{1}{2}$ lb potatoes, peeled, boiled and crushed
1 teaspoon vinegar	1 teaspoon vinegar
4 medium herrings	4 medium herrings
75 g/3 oz gram flour	$\frac{3}{4}$ cup gram flour
150 ml/$\frac{1}{4}$ pint water	$\frac{2}{3}$ cup water
1 tablespoon fresh breadcrumbs	1 tablespoon fresh soft bread crumbs
oil for deep frying	oil for deep frying
Garnish	*Garnish*
4 lettuce hearts	4 lettuce hearts
1 lemon, sliced	1 lemon, sliced
1 tablespoon chopped coriander leaves	1 tablespoon chopped coriander leaves

Heat the butter in a frying pan and fry the onion until golden. Add the cumin, ginger, salt, green chillies and coriander. Mix together with the lemon juice, crushed potato and vinegar.

Clean and gut the herrings and use the potato mixture to stuff them.

Make a batter by beating the gram flour, water and breadcrumbs together until smooth. Dip the fish in the batter to coat all over. Heat the oil until a day-old cube of bread turns golden in 1 minute. Fry the fish until golden and crisp on the outside. Garnish with the lettuce hearts, lemon slices and coriander leaves and serve hot.

Machchhi kabab
Haddock croquettes

Serves 4
Preparation time 25 minutes
Cooking time 20 minutes

This dish makes a marvellous light meal. It can also be served as a snack with tea or drinks. If preferred, the haddock can be replaced by cod or other white fish.

METRIC/IMPERIAL	AMERICAN
450 g/1 lb haddock fillet, steamed	1 lb haddock fillet, steamed
4 slices bread, soaked in water and squeezed dry	4 slices bread, soaked in water and squeezed dry
1 medium onion, chopped	1 medium onion, chopped
1 teaspoon grated root ginger	1 teaspoon grated root ginger
1 teaspoon garlic powder	1 teaspoon garlic powder
1 tablespoon chopped coriander leaves	1 tablespoon chopped coriander leaves
$\frac{1}{2}$ teaspoon freshly ground black pepper	$\frac{1}{2}$ teaspoon freshly ground black pepper
2 green chillies, finely chopped	2 green chilies, finely chopped
2 teaspoons salt	2 teaspoons salt
2 egg whites	2 egg whites
50 g/2 oz fresh breadcrumbs	1 cup fresh soft bread crumbs
oil for deep frying	oil for deep frying
tomato or mint sauce to serve	tomato or mint sauce to serve

Flake the haddock and mix with the soaked bread. Add the onion, ginger, garlic powder, coriander, pepper, chilli and salt and mix together to form a dough. Divide this dough into 16 portions and mould them to the required shape. Chill until firm.

Beat the egg white and coat each croquette with it. Roll the croquettes in the breadcrumbs to coat.

Heat the oil over a moderate heat until a day-old cube of bread turns golden in 1 minute. Deep fry 3 or 4 croquettes at a time until golden.

Serve sizzling hot with tomato or mint sauce.

Batakh-machhli ki tikki
Bombay duck bullets

Serves 4
Preparation time 20 minutes
Cooking time 15 minutes

Bombay duck is a fish the size of a herring found in abundance on the western seaboard of India, mainly around Bombay. This species has the unfishlike wont of swimming on the surface of the water, rather like a duck. Hence the soubriquet.
When raw, this fish smells foul – much more so than other fishes – but when cooked, it smells pleasant and tastes super. It is prepared in many different ways but is usually soaked, cleaned, cut and cured first. In the West it is available in cans. The fish can be baked in the oven and crumbled over a rice dish, or fried in fat, or, in fact, mixed with the other ingredients and converted into chops, cutlets or kababs.
It is a great appetiser, too!
The recipe given below is made at bullet speed. The concoction can be eaten as a teatime savoury or as a side dish with the main meal. Either way, it enlivens the meal.

METRIC/IMPERIAL	AMERICAN
10 canned Bombay ducks	10 canned Bombay ducks
225 g/8 oz mashed potato	1 cup mashed potato
$\frac{1}{2}$ teaspoon red chilli powder	$\frac{1}{2}$ teaspoon red chili powder
1 green chilli, finely chopped	1 green chili, finely chopped
1 teaspoon garam masala	1 teaspoon garam masala
1 teaspoon salt	1 teaspoon salt
1 medium onion, finely chopped	1 medium onion, finely chopped
Batter	*Batter*
225 g/$\frac{1}{2}$ lb gram flour	2 cups gram flour
300 ml/$\frac{1}{2}$ pint water	$1\frac{1}{4}$ cups water
oil for deep frying	oil for deep frying
tomato sauce to serve	tomato sauce to serve

Break the Bombay ducks into small pieces. Mix the potato, chilli powder, green chilli, garam masala, salt and onion and combine together thoroughly. Divide this mixture into eight portions and form into small bullet shapes.

Combine the batter ingredients to make a smooth mixture. Heat the oil over a moderate heat until a day-old cube of bread turns golden in 1 minute. Dip the bullets into the batter, one at a time, and deep fry in the oil until golden brown.

Serve hot with tomato sauce.

Litpiti machhli
Halibut yum yum

Serves 4
Preparation time 15 minutes
Cooking time 20 minutes

This dish, when prepared, should be moist. It can be eaten with chapatis, puris or paraunthas. If there is a curried dish on the menu, it can be eaten with rice as well.

METRIC/IMPERIAL	AMERICAN
100 g/4 oz ghee	$\frac{1}{2}$ cup ghee
1 large onion, chopped	1 large onion, chopped
1 green chilli, finely chopped	1 green chili, finely chopped
4 tomatoes, peeled and sliced	4 tomatoes, peeled and sliced
$1\frac{1}{2}$ teaspoons salt	$1\frac{1}{2}$ teaspoons salt
450 g/1 lb halibut, sliced	1 lb halibut, sliced
Spices	*Spices*
1 teaspoon turmeric powder	1 teaspoon turmeric powder
1 teaspoon coriander powder	1 teaspoon coriander powder
1 teaspoon paprika	1 teaspoon paprika pepper
1 teaspoon garam masala	1 teaspoon garam masala

Heat the ghee in a saucepan over a moderate heat. Add the onion and fry until golden brown. Stir in the turmeric, coriander, paprika and chilli, stir a few times then add the tomato, salt and fish. Mix well. Lower the heat, cover with a tightly fitting lid and simmer for 10 minutes.

Sprinkle with the garam masala and serve hot.

NOTE If the famous offering from the Kerala coast, that is, the halibut is not available, canned salmon can be used in its place.

Tali machhli
Fried fish

Serves 6
Preparation time 30 minutes
Cooking time 20 minutes

METRIC/IMPERIAL
900 g/2 lb white fish fillet
½ teaspoon turmeric powder
salt to taste
100 g/4 oz gram flour
450 ml/¾ pint water
2 tablespoons fresh breadcrumbs
½ teaspoon red chilli powder
½ teaspoon ground black pepper
2 tablespoons chopped coriander
leaves
1 green chilli, chopped
oil for deep frying
Garnish
2 tomatoes, sliced
1 lemon, sliced

AMERICAN
2 lb white fish fillet
½ teaspoon turmeric powder
salt to taste
1 cup gram flour
2 cups water
3 tablespoons fresh soft bread
crumbs
½ teaspoon red chili powder
½ teaspoon ground black pepper
3 tablespoons chopped coriander
leaves
1 green chili, chopped
oil for deep frying
Garnish
2 tomatoes, sliced
1 lemon, sliced

Wash the fish and cut into convenient-sized pieces. Rub the turmeric over the pieces with about 1 teaspoon salt and set aside for 10-15 minutes. Rinse the fish under cold running water.

Make a batter by mixing the gram flour, water, breadcrumbs, salt, chilli powder, black pepper, coriander and green chilli.

Heat the oil until a cube of day-old bread will brown in 1 minute. Meanwhile coat the fish with the batter. Fry the fish until golden all over, about 7-10 minutes.

Serve hot, garnished with tomato and lemon slices.

Right *Preparation for Nargisi kofta curry (see page 38).*
Overleaf *Plain rice pullao (see page 110); Nargisi kofta curry (see page 38); Cauliflower curry with yogurt (see page 83).*

Jheenga shorwedaar
Prawn curry

Serves 4
Preparation time 15 minutes
Cooking time 40 minutes

A rather expensive delicacy by Indian standards and a great favourite
with fish lovers.

METRIC/IMPERIAL	AMERICAN
4 tablespoons ghee	$\frac{1}{3}$ cup ghee
1 large onion, finely chopped	1 large onion, finely chopped
3 tablespoons coconut flour	$\frac{1}{4}$ cup coconut flour
15 g/$\frac{1}{2}$ oz ginger, grated	1 tablespoon grated ginger
2 green chillies, chopped	2 green chilies, chopped
salt to taste	salt to taste
1 teaspoon sugar	1 teaspoon sugar
2 tablespoons natural yogurt	3 tablespoons plain yogurt
1.15 litres/2 pints prawns, peeled	5 cups shrimps, shelled
300 ml/$\frac{1}{2}$ pint water	$1\frac{1}{4}$ cups water
Spices	*Spices*
5 cloves	5 cloves
5 green cardamoms	5 green cardamoms
5 bay leaves	5 bay leaves
$\frac{1}{2}$ teaspoon black cumin seeds	$\frac{1}{2}$ teaspoon black cumin seeds
1 teaspoon turmeric powder	1 teaspoon turmeric powder
$\frac{1}{2}$ teaspoon red chilli powder	$\frac{1}{2}$ teaspoon red chili powder

Heat the ghee in a saucepan and fry the onion until golden brown. Drain the onion and set aside.

Add the coconut flour, ginger and green chilli to the ghee remaining in the pan, together with all the spices. Fry gently for 2-3 minutes then stir in the salt, sugar and yogurt. Continue cooking for a few minutes then stir in the prawns. Cook over a low heat for 5 minutes, stirring continuously. Add the water, cover and leave to simmer for 20-25 minutes, or until the prawns are tender.

Serve hot, sprinkled with the hot fried onion.

Left *Duck curry (see page 52); Whole potatoes (see page 82).*

Machhli masaledaar
Plain fish curry

Serves 6
Preparation time 15 minutes
Cooking time 20 minutes

A dish in great demand in the Riparian restaurants. Bengalis are crazy about fish and are known for their excellent fish dishes.

METRIC/IMPERIAL	AMERICAN
675 g/1½ lb white fish fillet	1½ lb white fish fillet
100 g/4 oz ghee	½ cup ghee
2 medium onions	2 medium onions
4 cloves garlic, crushed	4 cloves garlic, crushed
15 g/½ oz ginger, crushed	1 tablespoon crushed ginger
4 tablespoons tomato purée	⅓ cup tomato paste
150 ml/¼ pint water	⅔ cup water
salt to taste	salt to taste
6 tomatoes, peeled and halved to garnish	6 tomatoes, peeled and halved to garnish
Spices	*Spices*
1 teaspoon white cumin seeds	1 teaspoon white cumin seeds
1 teaspoon turmeric powder	1 teaspoon turmeric powder
1 teaspoon garam masala	1 teaspoon garam masala

Cut the fish into medium-sized pieces. Heat the ghee in a frying pan and fry the fish gently for 5 minutes. Drain the fish on absorbent kitchen paper and set aside.

Chop one onion finely and grind the other one. Add the chopped onion to the ghee in the pan and fry until golden brown. Add all the spices and cook, stirring for about 10 seconds. Add the ground onion, garlic, ginger and tomato purée and fry the mixture until the ghee starts to separate.

Pour in the water and add salt to taste. Bring the mixture to the boil, remove from the heat and add the fried fish. Return to a low heat and simmer for 10 minutes.

Transfer the curry to a heated serving dish and garnish with the tomatoes.

Vegetarian soups

*Since southern India has always been predominantly vegetarian, the
first soups made were introduced to suit those needs.
Soups are often used in India as a substitute for a main course, per-
haps as a light meal for people convalescing after an illness.*

Shakahari ghoramghor
Vegetarian minestrone soup

Serves 4
Preparation time 10 minutes
Cooking time 25 minutes

METRIC/IMPERIAL	AMERICAN
25 g/1 oz ghee	2 tablespoons ghee
1 large onion, chopped	1 large onion, chopped
2 cloves garlic, crushed	2 cloves garlic, crushed
1 large carrot, diced	1 large carrot, diced
1 large turnip, diced	1 large turnip, diced
1 stick celery, chopped	1 stalk celery, chopped
2 tablespoons peas, fresh or frozen	3 tablespoons peas, fresh or frozen
100 g/4 oz white cabbage, shredded	$\frac{1}{4}$ lb white cabbage, shredded
4 large tomatoes, peeled and sliced	4 large tomatoes, peeled and sliced
2 teaspoons salt	2 teaspoons salt
900 ml/1$\frac{1}{2}$ pints water or vegetable stock	3$\frac{3}{4}$ cups water or vegetable stock
40 g/1$\frac{1}{2}$ oz spaghetti, broken in 2.5-cm/1-inch pieces	1$\frac{1}{2}$ oz spaghetti, broken in 1-inch pieces
$\frac{1}{2}$ teaspoon freshly ground black pepper	$\frac{1}{2}$ teaspoon freshly ground black pepper
1 tablespoon chopped coriander leaves to garnish	1 tablespoon chopped coriander leaves to garnish

Heat the ghee in a saucepan and fry the onion and garlic until golden. Add
the carrot, turnip, celery and peas and cook for 3 minutes. Stir in the
cabbage, tomato, salt and water and bring to the boil.

Lower the heat, add the spaghetti and pepper and simmer for 15 minutes.
Sprinkle the coriander over the soup before serving.

Adrak soup
Ginger soup

Serves 4
Preparation time 5 minutes
Cooking time 35 minutes

This is a rather unusual soup and you have to acquire a taste for it. It gives you inner warmth and is particularly good served on a cold winter's day.

METRIC/IMPERIAL	AMERICAN
25 g/1 oz root ginger, grated	2 tablespoons grated root ginger
900 ml/1½ pints water	3¾ cups water
1 teaspoon salt	1 teaspoon salt
1 tablespoon white cumin seeds, roasted and ground	1 tablespoon white cumin seeds, roasted and ground
½ teaspoon freshly ground black pepper	½ teaspoon freshly ground black pepper
juice of 1 lemon	juice of 1 lemon

Place the ginger in a saucepan, add the water and bring to the boil. Then leave it to simmer over a low heat for about 30 minutes until the water is reduced to half. Add the salt and cumin powder and leave for a further 2 minutes. Remove the pan from the heat, sprinkle with the pepper and pour a little lemon juice on each serving. Serve hot.

Kaddu soup
Pumpkin soup

Serves 4
Preparation time 10 minutes
Cooking time 35 minutes

METRIC/IMPERIAL	AMERICAN
450 g/1 lb pumpkin flesh, diced	1 lb pumpkin flesh, diced
1 large tomato, peeled and halved	1 large tomato, peeled and halved
1 large potato, halved	1 large potato, halved
300 ml/½ pint water or vegetable stock	1¼ cups water or vegetable stock
1 teaspoon salt	1 teaspoon salt
½ teaspoon freshly ground black pepper	½ teaspoon freshly ground black pepper
croûtons to serve (see page 30)	croûtons to serve (see page 30)

Place the pumpkin, tomato and potato together with water or stock in a saucepan and boil for 15 minutes. Add the salt and pepper and simmer over a moderate heat for a further 10 minutes, or until the vegetables are tender. Remove the pan from the heat, mash the vegetables to a purée or liquidise in an electric blender and then press the soup through a sieve.

Serve hot with croûtons.

Gobhi soup
Cauliflower soup

Serves 4
Preparation time 15 minutes
Cooking time 30 minutes

Cauliflowers are not usually associated with soup. As such, this dish may surprise you. But it tastes good, looks good and does you no harm.

METRIC/IMPERIAL	AMERICAN
1 small cauliflower, cut into florets	1 small head cauliflower, cut into florets
2 medium potatoes, diced	2 medium potatoes, diced
1½ teaspoons salt	1½ teaspoons salt
600 ml/1 pint water	2½ cups water
1 tablespoon oil	1 tablespoon oil
1 medium onion, chopped	1 medium onion, chopped
4 medium tomatoes, peeled and chopped	4 medium tomatoes, peeled and chopped
50 g/2 oz butter	¼ cup butter
1 teaspoon chopped coriander leaves	1 teaspoon chopped coriander leaves
½ teaspoon freshly ground black pepper	½ teaspoon freshly ground black pepper

Place the cauliflower and potato together with the salt and water in a saucepan. Cook over a moderate heat for 20 minutes. Remove the pan from the heat, strain the liquid into a large bowl and mash the contents from the strainer in another bowl.

Now heat the oil in a deep frying pan and fry the onions until golden. Slowly pour the strained liquid and the mashed vegetables into the pan, together with the tomato and mix thoroughly. Cook for a further 10 minutes over a moderate heat.

Cut the butter into four cubes and add one, with coriander and a pinch of pepper to each serving. Serve piping hot.

Moong dall soup
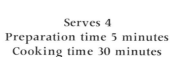
Split green bean soup

Serves 4
Preparation time 5 minutes
Cooking time 30 minutes

METRIC/IMPERIAL	AMERICAN
225 g/8 oz split green beans, skins removed	1 cup split green beans, skins removed
900 ml/1½ pints water	3¾ cups water
1½ teaspoons salt	1½ teaspoons salt
1 teaspoon turmeric powder	1 teaspoon turmeric powder
225 g/8 oz tomatoes, peeled and sliced	½ lb tomatoes, peeled and sliced
2 tablespoons ghee or butter	3 tablespoons ghee or butter
1 medium onion, finely chopped	1 medium onion, finely chopped
½ teaspoon freshly ground black pepper	½ teaspoon freshly ground black pepper
1½ teaspoons lemon juice	1½ teaspoons lemon juice

Clean and drain the beans several times. Then place the drained beans together with the water in a pan and bring to the boil over a moderate heat. Add the salt and turmeric powder and leave uncovered to simmer for about 15 minutes. Remove the scum from the top after the first boiling.

When the beans are tender, add the tomato, lower the heat and cook for a further 10 minutes.

While the mixture is cooking, heat the ghee in a frying pan and fry the onion until golden. Remove and reserve on a separate plate.

When the soup is cooked, add the pepper and stir a few times. Transfer the contents into four individual dishes and serve with a sprinkling of the reserved onions and a few drops of lemon juice.

Dall
Pulses or legumes

*Pulses are an institution in India and are an essential part of the
kachcha vegetarian meal. They are widely used for their good flavour
and food value.*

Toor dall
Pigeon pea purée

Serves 4
Preparation time 15 minutes
Cooking time 1 hour

*A vegetarian kachcha meal is incomplete without a dall. This is one of
the most popular – eat it with chapatis or rice.*

METRIC/IMPERIAL	AMERICAN
175 g/6 oz ghee	$\frac{3}{4}$ cup ghee
6 cloves garlic, crushed	6 cloves garlic, crushed
2 medium onions, crushed	2 medium onions, crushed
225 g/8 oz pigeon peas	1 cup pigeon peas
900 ml/1$\frac{1}{2}$ pints water	3$\frac{3}{4}$ cups water
salt to taste	salt to taste
1 green mango, peeled and sliced	1 green mango, peeled and sliced
1 green chilli, chopped	1 green chili, chopped
2 tablespoons chopped coriander	3 tablespoons chopped coriander
leaves to garnish	leaves to garnish
Spices	*Spices*
1 teaspoon turmeric powder	1 teaspoon turmeric powder
1 teaspoon white cumin seeds	1 teaspoon white cumin seeds
pinch of asafoetida powder	dash of asafoetida powder
$\frac{1}{2}$ teaspoon red chilli powder	$\frac{1}{2}$ teaspoon red chili powder

Heat one-third of the ghee in a saucepan and fry the garlic and half the onion
until golden brown. Stir in the turmeric, pigeon peas, water and salt to taste.
Simmer, covered, for about 30 minutes.

Add the mango slices to the pigeon pea mixture and cook for a further 15-20
minutes. Transfer the mixture to a casserole dish and keep hot.

Heat the remaining ghee and fry the rest of the onion with the cumin until
golden brown. Remove from the heat and add the green chilli, asafoetida and
red chilli powder. Mix well and pour over the dall mixture in the casserole.
Serve hot, garnished with the coriander.

Saag-pahete
Spinach in skinless black beans

Serves 6
Preparation time 15 minutes
Cooking time 1¾ hours

This dish gives body and muscle to a dall mixture and pleases Popeye
fans no end!

METRIC/IMPERIAL	AMERICAN
900 ml/1½ pints water	3¾ cups water
salt to taste	salt to taste
225 g/8 oz skinless dried black beans	1 cup skinless dried black beans
450 g/1 lb spinach, coarsely chopped	1 lb spinach, coarsely chopped
15 g/½ oz root ginger, grated	1 tablespoon grated root ginger
100 g/4 oz ghee	½ cup ghee
1 medium onion, chopped	1 medium onion, chopped
10 cloves garlic, crushed	10 cloves garlic, crushed
50 g/2 oz butter	¼ cup butter
Spices	*Spices*
½ teaspoon turmeric powder	½ teaspoon turmeric powder
2 dry red chillies	2 dry red chilies
1 teaspoon white cumin seeds	1 teaspoon white cumin seeds

Boil the water in a saucepan and add the salt, beans and turmeric. Simmer, stirring occasionally, for 1 hour.

Add the spinach, ginger and red chillies and cook for a further 30 minutes.

Heat the ghee in a frying pan and fry the onion, garlic and cumin until golden brown. Pour over the dall mixture and cook together for 10 minutes. Melt the butter and pour a little over each helping.

Chhili urad dall
Skinless split black beans

Serves 4
Preparation time 15 minutes
Cooking time 50 minutes

Some people like their dalls to have a thin consistency—I do not. The
beauty of this preparation is that it remains thick and all the dall
seeds separate. Serve with melted ghee, chapatis and rice.

METRIC/IMPERIAL	AMERICAN
225 g/8 oz skinless dried black beans	1 cup skinless dried black beans
salt to taste	salt to taste
600 ml/1 pint water	2½ cups water
100 g/4 oz ghee	½ cup ghee
1 medium onion, finely chopped	1 medium onion, finely chopped
2 cloves garlic, crushed	2 cloves garlic, crushed
1 green chilli, chopped	1 green chili, chopped
Spices	*Spices*
½ teaspoon turmeric powder	½ teaspoon turmeric powder
1 teaspoon white cumin seeds	1 teaspoon white cumin seeds
pinch of asafoetida powder	dash of asafoetida powder
1 dry red chilli, crushed	1 dry red chili, crushed

Mix the beans, salt, turmeric and water together in a saucepan and simmer
until the water is all absorbed, about 45 minutes.

Heat the ghee in a frying pan and fry the onion, garlic and cumin until
golden brown. Stir in the asafoetida and green and red chillies.

Divide the dall mixture between four individual bowls and spoon a quarter
of the onion mixture over each one. Serve hot.

Masoor ki dall
Lentils

Serves 6
Preparation time 15 minutes
Cooking time 2 hours

There is a saying in Hindi which means that you have to have a special mouth before you are entitled to share the experience of eating this dall.

METRIC/IMPERIAL	AMERICAN
225 g/8 oz lentils	1 cup lentils
1.15 litres/2 pints water	5 cups water
salt to taste	salt to taste
175 g/6 oz ghee	$\frac{3}{4}$ cup ghee
1 large onion, chopped	1 large onion, chopped
1 green chilli, chopped	1 green chilli, chopped
Spices	*Spices*
$\frac{1}{2}$ teaspoon red chilli powder	$\frac{1}{2}$ teaspoon red chili powder
1 teaspoon white cumin seeds	1 teaspoon white cumin seeds
pinch of asafoetida powder	dash of asafoetida powder

Wash the lentils in cold, running water, drain then add to the measured water in a saucepan with salt to taste. Simmer for $1\frac{1}{2}$ hours.

Heat one-third of the ghee in a separate saucepan and fry the onion until golden brown. Add the green chilli and red chilli powder and stir the onion mixture into the cooked lentils. Simmer for a further 10 minutes.

Heat the remaining ghee with the cumin and asafoetida powder for about 30 seconds then pour about 1 tablespoon over each serving.

Chana urad dall
Gram and black bean dall

Serves 6
Preparation time 15 minutes
Cooking time 2 hours

This recipe gives a thick dall.

METRIC/IMPERIAL	AMERICAN
1.15 litres/2 pints water	5 cups water
100 g/4 oz split grams	$\frac{1}{2}$ cup split grams
100 g/4 oz skinless dried black beans	$\frac{1}{2}$ cup skinless dried black beans
salt to taste	salt to taste
100 g/4 oz marrow flesh	$\frac{1}{4}$ lb zucchini squash flesh
100 g/4 oz ghee	$\frac{1}{2}$ cup ghee
1 medium onion, finely chopped	1 medium onion, finely chopped
6 cloves garlic, crushed	6 cloves garlic, crushed
1 green chilli, chopped	1 green chili, chopped
Spices	*Spices*
$\frac{1}{2}$ teaspoon turmeric powder	$\frac{1}{2}$ teaspoon turmeric powder
1 teaspoon white cumin seeds	1 teaspoon white cumin seeds
1 dry red chilli, crushed	1 dry red chili, crushed
$\frac{1}{2}$ teaspoon red chilli powder	$\frac{1}{2}$ teaspoon red chili powder

Boil the water in a saucepan. Wash the grams and beans under cold, running water and drain. Add to the boiling water with the salt and turmeric. Bring to the boil then cover and simmer for $1\frac{1}{2}$ hours, stirring occasionally.

Cut the marrow into 5-cm/2-inch pieces and add to the dall mixture. Simmer for a further 30 minutes.

Heat the ghee in a frying pan and fry the onion, garlic and cumin until golden brown. Remove from the heat and add the crushed and powdered red and chopped green chillies. Transfer this mixture to a small stainless steel bowl and sprinkle over the dall mixture when served.

Kabab allahabadi
Chick chops

Serves 6
Preparation time 8½ hours
Cooking time 30 minutes

METRIC/IMPERIAL
450 g/1 lb chick peas
900 ml/1½ pints water
1 large onion, chopped
50 g/2 oz root ginger, coarsely chopped
10 cloves garlic, crushed
2½ teaspoons salt
1 medium onion, finely chopped
2 green chillies, finely chopped
1 (3.5-cm/1½-inch) piece root ginger, grated
2 tablespoons chopped coriander leaves
beaten egg to bind
100 g/4 oz ghee
2 lemons, sliced to garnish
sweet or sour sauce to serve
Spices
2 tablespoons coriander seeds
1 teaspoon red chilli powder
6 cloves
2 teaspoons brown cardamom seeds
10 black peppercorns
½ teaspoon black cumin seeds
½ teaspoon white cumin seeds
2 (5-cm/2-inch) pieces cinnamon stick
½ teaspoon green cardamom seeds
½ teaspoon ground mace
½ teaspoon grated nutmeg

AMERICAN
2¼ cups chick peas
3¾ cups water
1 large onion, chopped
⅓ cup coarsely chopped root ginger
10 cloves garlic, crushed
2½ teaspoons salt
1 medium onion, finely chopped
2 green chilies, finely chopped
1 (1½-inch) piece root ginger, grated
3 tablespoons chopped coriander leaves
beaten egg to bind
½ cup ghee
2 lemons, sliced to garnish
sweet or sour sauce to serve
Spices
3 tablespoons coriander seeds
1 teaspoon red chili powder
6 cloves
2 teaspoons brown cardamom seeds
10 black peppercorns
½ teaspoon black cumin seeds
½ teaspoon white cumin seeds
2 (2-inch) pieces cinnamon stick
½ teaspoon green cardamom seeds
½ teaspoon ground mace
½ teaspoon grated nutmeg

Soak the chick peas overnight in water. Remove any which have not softened and discard them. Drain the chick peas and mix with the measured water, onion, ginger, garlic and salt together with all the spices and bring to the boil. When the chick peas are tender enough to crush between the thumb and finger, remove from the heat and leave to cool. Drain off any excess water and grind the remaining mixture. Mix in the onion, green chilli, ginger, coriander and beaten egg and divide into 18 portions. Form into round cakes.

  Heat the ghee in a frying pan and fry the chick chops on both sides until golden brown. Garnish with slices of lemon and serve with a sauce of your choice.

Shorwedaar, bhaji and bharwan tarkariyan
Curried, fried and stuffed vegetables

*Most of the dishes here are accompaniments to a main course in
kachcha and pukka meals.
Bhajis and mussallams lend extra variety to a meal as do the stuffed
vegetables; all contribute to give an Indian meal flavour and texture.*

Torai do-piazza
Courgette and onion

Serves 4
Preparation time 10 minutes
Cooking time 25 minutes

*This dish is moist when cooked and is delicious eaten with any of the
breads. It can also be eaten with a rice dish, provided that it is
accompanied by a curry.*

METRIC/IMPERIAL	AMERICAN
900 g/2 lb courgettes	2 lb zucchini
2 tablespoons ghee	3 tablespoons ghee
450 g/1 lb large onions, thinly sliced	1 lb large onions, thinly sliced
2 cloves garlic, crushed	2 cloves garlic, crushed
1 green chilli, chopped or 1 teaspoon red chilli powder	1 green chili, chopped or 1 teaspoon red chili powder
1½ teaspoons salt	1½ teaspoons salt

Clean and peel the courgettes and cut into 2.5-cm/1-inch pieces.

Heat the ghee in a saucepan over a moderate heat. Add half the onion and all
the garlic and fry until light brown. Mix in the chilli or chilli powder and
cook for a few minutes, stirring. Add the salt and courgettes and cook for
about 5 minutes, stirring continuously.

Now add the rest of the onions and stir well. Reduce the heat, cover and
leave to simmer for about 15 minutes.

Serve hot with puris or paraunthas.

Dum aloo
Whole potatoes

Serves 6
Preparation time 2½ hours
Cooking time 1 hour

METRIC/IMPERIAL

900 g/2 lb round new potatoes
900 ml/1½ pints water
2 teaspoons salt
ghee or oil for deep frying
225 g/8 oz ghee
1 large onion, finely chopped
4 tablespoons tomato purée
1 (142-ml/5-fl oz) carton natural
yogurt
4 tablespoons hot water
1 green pepper, seeds removed and
sliced
1 teaspoon garam masala
Spices
4 cloves
4 bay leaves
6 black peppercorns
4 green cardamoms
1 brown cardamom
1 (5-cm/2-inch) piece cinnamon stick
Paste
1 large onion, chopped
12 cloves garlic, crushed
25 g/1 oz root ginger, crushed
6 black peppercorns
4 cloves
1 (5-cm/2-inch) piece cinnamon stick
1 brown cardamom
1 teaspoon poppy seeds
1 tablespoon coriander seeds
1 teaspoon black cumin seeds
2 dry red chillies
1 teaspoon turmeric powder
pinch of ground mace
pinch of grated nutmeg

AMERICAN

2 lb round new potatoes
3¾ cups water
2 teaspoons salt
ghee or oil for deep frying
1 cup ghee
1 large onion, finely chopped
⅓ cup tomato paste
1 (5-fl oz) carton plain yogurt
⅓ cup hot water
1 green pepper, seeds removed and
sliced
1 teaspoon garam masala
Spices
4 cloves
4 bay leaves
6 black peppercorns
4 green cardamoms
1 brown cardamom
1 (2-inch) piece cinnamon stick
Paste
1 large onion, chopped
12 cloves garlic, crushed
2 tablespoons crushed root ginger
6 black peppercorns
4 cloves
1 (2-inch) piece cinnamon stick
1 brown cardamom
1 teaspoon poppy seeds
1 tablespoon coriander seeds
1 teaspoon black cumin seeds
2 dry red chilies
1 teaspoon turmeric powder
dash of ground mace
dash of grated nutmeg

Scrape the potatoes, prick all over with a fork and soak in the water with half the salt for 2 hours. Dry the potatoes on a cloth and heat the ghee or oil until a cube of day-old bread turns golden in 1 minute. Deep fry the potatoes until golden brown. Drain and set aside.

Heat the measured ghee in a flameproof casserole and fry the onion with all the spices until golden. Grind the paste ingredients to a fairly smooth mixture and stir into the onion. Cook for 10 minutes. Stir in the tomato purée, yogurt and remaining salt

Add the potatoes and hot water and stir over a low heat for 5 minutes. Sprinkle with the pepper and garam masala and cook in a moderate oven (180°C, 350°F, Gas Mark 4) for 20 minutes.

Khatti gobhi rasedaar
Cauliflower curry with yogurt

Serves 6
Preparation time 15 minutes
Cooking time 50 minutes

METRIC/IMPERIAL	AMERICAN
675 g/1½ lb cauliflower	1½ lb head of cauliflower
100 g/4 oz ghee	½ cup ghee
2 (142 ml/5 fl oz) cartons natural yogurt	2 (5-fl oz) cartons plain yogurt
2 large onions, finely chopped	2 large onions, finely chopped
2 cloves garlic, crushed	2 cloves garlic, crushed
salt to taste	salt to taste
4 bay leaves	4 bay leaves
300 ml/½ pint hot water	1¼ cups hot water
2 tablespoons chopped coriander leaves to garnish	3 tablespoons chopped coriander leaves to garnish
Spices	*Spices*
pinch of asafoetida powder	dash of asafoetida powder
6 cloves	6 cloves
6 black peppercorns	6 black peppercorns
1 brown cardamom	1 brown cardamom
2 green cardamoms	2 green cardamoms
2 (2.5-cm/1-inch) pieces cinnamon stick	2 (1-inch) pieces cinnamon stick
1 teaspoon coriander seeds	1 teaspoon coriander seeds
1 teaspoon white cumin seeds	1 teaspoon white cumin seeds
1 teaspoon red chilli powder	1 teaspoon red chili powder

Cut the cauliflower into florets. Heat a quarter of the ghee in a saucepan with the asafoetida and add the cauliflower. Cook for 5 minutes, drain the cauliflower and pour over the yogurt.

Heat the remaining ghee and fry the onion, garlic, salt, bay leaves and all the spices except the chilli powder until golden. Add the chilli powder, cauliflower and yogurt and cook over a low heat for 10 minutes. Add the water and simmer for 25 minutes. Serve sprinkled with coriander.

Kathal shorwedaar
Jackfruit curry

Serves 6
Preparation time 25 minutes
Cooking time 1 hour

Jackfruit is not a vegetable which is easily available in the markets of the West, but it does appear in the greengrocer's shops from time to time. When found and cooked, however, the dish tastes out of this world.

METRIC/IMPERIAL	AMERICAN
900 g/2 lb baby jackfruit	2 lb baby jackfruit
225 g/8 oz ghee	1 cup ghee
1 medium onion, finely chopped	1 medium onion, finely chopped
4 bay leaves	4 bay leaves
6 tablespoons tomato purée	$\frac{1}{2}$ cup tomato paste
4 tablespoons natural yogurt	$\frac{1}{3}$ cup plain yogurt
300 ml/$\frac{1}{2}$ pint water	$1\frac{1}{4}$ cups water
salt to taste	salt to taste
Paste	*Paste*
1 medium onion, chopped	1 medium onion, chopped
8 cloves garlic, crushed	8 cloves garlic, crushed
15 g/$\frac{1}{2}$ oz root ginger, crushed	1 tablespoon crushed root ginger
1 tablespoon coriander seeds	1 tablespoon coriander seeds
Spices	*Spices*
4 cloves	4 cloves
4 black peppercorns	4 black peppercorns
1 brown cardamom	1 brown cardamom
2 green cardamoms	2 green cardamoms
1 teaspoon turmeric powder	1 teaspoon turmeric powder
1 teaspoon red chilli powder	1 teaspoon red chili powder
1 tablespoon garam masala	1 tablespoon garam masala

Using a greased knife and greased hands, clean the jackfruit and cut it into medium-sized pieces.

Heat the ghee in a flameproof casserole and fry the jackfruit with the first four spices until golden brown. Drain the jackfruit and set aside.

Fry the onions in the ghee left in the pan until golden and add the bay leaves, tomato purée, yogurt and turmeric and chilli powders. Make a fairly smooth mixture by grinding all the paste ingredients together and add this to the pan. Cook all together over a low heat until the ghee starts to separate.

Add the jackfruit and cook, stirring, for 5 minutes. Stir in the water and salt and bring to the boil. Transfer the dish to a moderate oven (180°C, 350°F, Gas Mark 4) for about 1 hour or until the jackfruit is tender. Sprinkle with garam masala before serving.

Right *Cauliflower soup (see page 73); Pumpkin soup (see page 72).*

Matar paneer
Cream cheese and pea curry

Serves 4
Preparation time 20 minutes
Cooking time 45 minutes

Although this is a speciality of the Punjab region, it is cooked universally. This is a dainty dish which truly enhances a meatless meal. Serve with any bread or rice dishes.

METRIC/IMPERIAL	AMERICAN
2 medium onions, chopped	2 medium onions, chopped
6 cloves garlic, crushed	6 cloves garlic, crushed
1 tablespoon coriander seeds	1 tablespoon coriander seeds
100 g/4 oz ghee	$\frac{1}{2}$ cup ghee
225 g/8 oz paneer (see page 22)	$\frac{1}{2}$ lb paneer (see page 22)
15 g/$\frac{1}{2}$ oz root ginger, grated	1 tablespoon grated root ginger
4 bay leaves	4 bay leaves
1 teaspoon turmeric powder	1 teaspoon turmeric powder
450 g/1 lb peas, shelled	1 lb peas, shelled
1 (142-ml/5-fl oz) carton natural yogurt	1 (5-fl oz) carton plain yogurt
2 green chillies, chopped	2 green chilies, chopped
225 g/8 oz tomatoes, peeled and sliced	$\frac{1}{2}$ lb tomatoes, peeled and sliced
salt to taste	salt to taste
450 ml/$\frac{3}{4}$ pint water	2 cups water
Garnish	*Garnish*
garam masala	garam masala
2 tablespoons chopped coriander leaves	3 tablespoons chopped coriander leaves

Make a paste by grinding together half the onions, the garlic and coriander seeds.

Heat the ghee in a frying pan and cut the paneer into 2.5-cm/1-inch cubes. Fry the paneer to a light brown and remove to drain on a plate.

Add the remaining onion and the ginger to the ghee in the pan, add the bay leaves and fry until the onion is golden brown. Add the turmeric and the paste mixture and fry until the ghee starts to separate.

Add the cheese and peas along with the yogurt, chilli, tomato and salt. Stir for 5-6 minutes over a low heat.

Pour in the water and simmer gently for 20 minutes. Serve sprinkled with garam masala and coriander.

Previous page: *A Pukka Vegetarian Meal – Flattened artichokes (see page 98); Puri stuffed with dall (see page 117); Marrow kofta curry (see page 94); Pappadums (see page 130).*
Left *Chick chops (see page 80); Skinless split black beans (see page 77).*

Gobhi-aloo-matar
Cauliflower, potato and pea curry

Serves 4
Preparation time 15 minutes
Cooking time 1 hour

A delicious curry if you like this vegetable combination. Experiment
with alternative vegetables too.

METRIC/IMPERIAL	AMERICAN
100 g/4 oz ghee	$\frac{1}{2}$ cup ghee
1 small cauliflower, cut in florets	1 small head cauliflower, cut in florets
450 g/1 lb potatoes, quartered	1 lb potatoes, quartered
100 g/4 oz shelled peas	1 cup shelled peas
1 medium onion, finely chopped	1 medium onion, finely chopped
450 g/1 lb tomatoes, peeled and thinly sliced	1 lb tomatoes, peeled and thinly sliced
450 ml/$\frac{3}{4}$ pint water	2 cups water
salt to taste	salt to taste
Spices	*Spices*
pinch of asafoetida powder	dash of asafoetida powder
2 cloves	2 cloves
1 teaspoon white cumin seeds	1 teaspoon white cumin seeds
1 brown cardamom	1 brown cardamom
Paste	*Paste*
1 medium onion, chopped	1 medium onion, chopped
4 cloves garlic, crushed	4 cloves garlic, crushed
1 (2.5-cm/1-inch) piece root ginger, crushed	1 (1-inch) piece root ginger, crushed
1 teaspoon turmeric powder	1 teaspoon turmeric powder
1 teaspoon red chilli powder	1 teaspoon red chili powder
1 tablespoon roasted coriander seeds	1 tablespoon roasted coriander seeds
$\frac{1}{2}$ teaspoon ground cinnamon	$\frac{1}{2}$ teaspoon ground cinnamon
Garnish	*Garnish*
1 teaspoon garam masala	1 teaspoon garam masala
2 tablespoons chopped coriander leaves	3 tablespoons chopped coriander leaves

Heat one-quarter of the ghee in a saucepan and add the asafoetida powder. Stir for 5 seconds then add the cauliflower, potato and peas. Fry for 5 minutes over a moderate heat. Remove the vegetables to a plate and set aside.

Heat the remaining ghee and add the onion, cloves, cumin and cardamom and fry until the onion is golden brown.

Make a fairly smooth mixture by grinding all the paste ingredients together. Add the paste to the onion mixture and cook until the ghee starts to separate.

Mix in the fried vegetables and tomato and fry for 5 minutes, stirring occasionally. Stir in the water and salt and simmer for 30 minutes.

Serve hot, garnished with the garam masala and coriander.

Navratan tarkasi
Cocktail curry

Serves 4
Preparation time 35 minutes
Cooking time 40 minutes

This is the choicest vegetable curry. It caters for all vegetarian preferences as the specified vegetables can, of course, be altered or substituted. The famous South Indian dish, Aviyal, is made in the same way, by simply mashing the flesh of a coconut to a purée with the milk from the shell and adding it to the mixture with the green chillies.

METRIC/IMPERIAL	AMERICAN
50 g/2 oz butter	$\frac{1}{4}$ cup butter
1 onion, chopped	1 onion, chopped
1 teaspoon white cumin seeds	1 teaspoon white cumin seeds
225 g/8 oz potatoes, cubed	$\frac{1}{2}$ lb potatoes, cubed
1 small cauliflower, cut in florets	1 small head cauliflower, cut in florets
1 small aubergine, peeled and coarsely chopped	1 small eggplant, peeled and coarsely chopped
100 g/4 oz shelled peas	1 cup shelled peas
450 g/1 lb tomatoes, peeled and quartered	1 lb tomatoes, peeled and quartered
100 g/4 oz carrots, chopped	$\frac{1}{4}$ lb carrots, chopped
1 small turnip, chopped	1 small turnip, chopped
small bunch spring onions, chopped	small bunch scallions, chopped
100 g/4 oz marrow flesh, chopped	$\frac{1}{4}$ lb zucchini squash flesh, chopped
1 (142-ml/5-fl oz) carton natural yogurt	1 (5-fl oz) carton plain yogurt
150 ml/$\frac{1}{4}$ pint water	$\frac{2}{3}$ cup water
salt to taste	salt to taste
2 green chillies, finely chopped	2 green chilies, finely chopped
1 teaspoon garam masala	1 teaspoon garam masala
1 tablespoon chopped coriander leaves to garnish	1 tablespoon chopped coriander leaves to garnish

Heat the butter in a saucepan and fry the onion with the cumin until golden brown. Stir in all the prepared vegetables and cook, stirring for 5 minutes. Mix the yogurt and water together and stir into the curry. Add the salt, green chilli and garam masala and cook, stirring, for 2-3 minutes. Cover and simmer gently for 30 minutes. Serve hot, garnished with the coriander.

Matar keema
Minced peas

Serves 4
Preparation time 20 minutes
Cooking time 30 minutes

I am sure this vegetarian dish will find favour with non-vegetarians too. It is a moist and exquisite dish – a great favourite of mine. Serve it with a rice pullao or one of the breads. Papad, pickles or chutney would be its usual accompaniments.

METRIC/IMPERIAL	AMERICAN
100 g/4 oz ghee	$\frac{1}{2}$ cup ghee
1 teaspoon grated root ginger	1 teaspoon grated root ginger
275 g/10 oz peas, coarsely ground	$1\frac{3}{4}$ cups peas, coarsely ground
2 medium potatoes, finely chopped	2 medium potatoes, finely chopped
2 bay leaves	2 bay leaves
2 onions, chopped	2 onions, chopped
2 medium tomatoes, peeled and halved	2 medium tomatoes, peeled and halved
2 teaspoons salt	2 teaspoons salt
300 ml/$\frac{1}{2}$ pint water	$1\frac{1}{4}$ cups water
Paste	*Paste*
6 cloves garlic, crushed	6 cloves garlic, crushed
15 g/$\frac{1}{2}$ oz root ginger, grated	1 tablespoon grated root ginger
$1\frac{1}{2}$ teaspoons turmeric powder	$1\frac{1}{2}$ teaspoons turmeric powder
$1\frac{1}{2}$ teaspoons red chilli powder	$1\frac{1}{2}$ teaspoons red chili powder
$1\frac{1}{2}$ tablespoons coriander seeds	$1\frac{1}{2}$ tablespoons coriander seeds
Garnish	*Garnish*
1 tablespoon chopped coriander leaves	1 tablespoon chopped coriander leaves
$1\frac{1}{2}$ teaspoons garam masala	$1\frac{1}{2}$ teaspoons garam masala

First make a smooth mixture by grinding all the paste ingredients together.

Heat 1 tablespoon of the ghee in a frying pan over a low heat. Add the ginger and peas. Fry gently for 5 minutes until the grains of the peas start to separate. Remove and set aside.

Add another tablespoon of the ghee to the pan and fry the potato for 5 minutes. Remove and mix with the peas.

Heat the remaining ghee, add the bay leaves and onion and fry until golden brown. Reduce the heat and stir in the tomatoes and paste. Cook for 10 minutes, stirring occasionally. When the ghee starts to separate add the pea and potato mixture with the salt. Cook, stirring, for 5 minutes, add the water then cover and simmer for 15 minutes. Serve sprinkled with the coriander and garam masala.

Chane paani
Gram and water curry

Serves 6
Preparation time 15 minutes plus overnight soak
Cooking time 1½ hours

Once you have acquired a taste for this dish, its memory will always be with you.

METRIC/IMPERIAL	AMERICAN
450 g/1 lb grams or pigeon peas	2 cups grams or pigeon peas
100 g/4 oz ghee	½ cup ghee
2 medium onions, finely chopped	2 medium onions, finely chopped
1 teaspoon turmeric powder	1 teaspoon turmeric powder
1 teaspoon garam masala	1 teaspoon garam masala
4 cloves garlic, crushed	4 cloves garlic, crushed
1 teaspoon grated root ginger	1 teaspoon grated root ginger
2 green chillies, finely chopped	2 green chilies, finely chopped
2 (142-ml/5-fl oz) cartons natural yogurt	2 (5-fl oz) cartons plain yogurt
1 teaspoon lemon juice	1 teaspoon lemon juice
450 ml/¾ pint water	2 cups water
salt to taste	salt to taste

Soak the grams or pigeon peas overnight in cold water. Rinse under running water, drain and divide them into two portions. Crush half and leave the rest whole.

Heat the ghee in a saucepan and fry the onion until golden brown. Stir in the turmeric, garam masala, garlic, ginger and chillies. Add both portions of grams and stir well. After 5 minutes add the yogurt and lemon juice. Stir over a moderate heat for 5 minutes.

Mix in the water with salt to taste. Cover and simmer for 1 hour. Serve hot with chapatis, puris, paraunthas, rice or side dishes.

Lauki kofte
Marrow kofta curry

Serves 4
Preparation time $1\frac{1}{2}$ hours
Cooking time 45 minutes

Another masterpiece from the culinary repertoire of the vegetable kofta artistes! A truly delightful dish for a discerning guest.

METRIC/IMPERIAL	AMERICAN
450 g/1 lb marrow flesh	1 lb zucchini squash flesh
4 tablespoons gram flour	$\frac{1}{3}$ cup gram flour
salt to taste	salt to taste
15 g/$\frac{1}{2}$ oz root ginger, grated	1 tablespoon grated root ginger
2 green chillies, finely chopped	2 green chilies, finely chopped
225 g/8 oz ghee	1 cup ghee
2 medium onions, finely chopped	2 medium onions, finely chopped
2 bay leaves	2 bay leaves
225 g/8 oz tomatoes, peeled and sliced	$\frac{1}{2}$ lb tomatoes, peeled and sliced
300 ml/$\frac{1}{2}$ pint water	$1\frac{1}{4}$ cups water
Spices	*Spices*
2 teaspoons garam masala	2 teaspoons garam masala
1 brown cardamom	1 brown cardamom
4 cloves	4 cloves
Paste	*Paste*
1 medium onion, chopped	1 medium onion, chopped
4 cloves garlic, crushed	4 cloves garlic, crushed
1 teaspoon white cumin seeds	1 teaspoon white cumin seeds
1 teaspoon turmeric powder	1 teaspoon turmeric powder

Grate the marrow and mix with the gram flour, 1 teaspoon of the garam masala, about 1 teaspoon salt, the ginger and green chilli. Form the mixture into small balls. Chill on absorbent kitchen paper for 2 hours.

Heat the ghee in a saucepan and fry the balls until golden brown. Drain and set aside.

Add the onion to the ghee remaining in the pan with the bay leaves, cardamom and cloves. Fry until the onion is golden brown.

Grind the paste ingredients together until fairly smooth then add to the onion mixture and cook for 5-7 minutes, stirring occasionally, until the ghee starts to separate.

Stir in the tomatoes and salt to taste and mix in the water. Drop in the fried marrow balls and heat through gently in the sauce. Sprinkle with the remaining garam masala 5 minutes before serving.

Dhoka
Delusion fritters

Serves 4
Preparation time 20 minutes
Cooking time 35 minutes

This is a remarkable dish in that the fritters can be used as a snack or side dish and can be curried too. They are most enjoyable as a teatime savoury – I used to love them as a child and still do to this day.

METRIC/IMPERIAL	AMERICAN
2 green chillies, finely chopped	2 green chilies, finely chopped
1 teaspoon baking powder	1 teaspoon baking powder
2 medium onions chopped	2 medium onions, chopped
15 g/½ oz root ginger, grated	1 tablespoon grated root ginger
salt to taste	salt to taste
8 cloves garlic, crushed	8 cloves garlic, crushed
450 g/1 lb gram flour	4 cups gram flour
250 ml/8 fl oz water	1 cup water
100 g/4 oz ghee	½ cup ghee
2 teaspoons lemon juice	2 teaspoons lemon juice
2 tablespoons chopped coriander leaves	3 tablespoons chopped coriander leaves
Spices	*Spices*
1 teaspoon garam masala	1 teaspoon garam masala
1 teaspoon carom seeds	1 teaspoon carom seeds
1 teaspoon white cumin seeds	1 teaspoon white cumin seeds
½ teaspoon turmeric powder	½ teaspoon turmeric powder
1 teaspoon red chilli powder	1 teaspoon red chili powder
1 teaspoon ground coriander	1 teaspoon ground coriander

Mix together the chillies, baking powder, half the onion, the ginger, salt, garlic, gram flour, the first three spices and the water. Knead the mixture thoroughly and shape into eight equal sausage shapes, about 2.5 cm/1 inch in diameter.

Boil a saucepan of water and cook the sausage shapes in it for 10-15 minutes then drain, discarding the water. Allow the sausages to cool then cut into 1-cm/½-inch slices.

Heat the ghee in a frying pan and fry the remaining onion until golden brown. Add the remaining spices and stir well. Add the sausage slices and stir over a low heat for 10 minutes, taking care not to break the pieces.

Pour over the lemon juice and sprinkle with the coriander before serving.

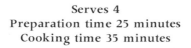

Bundgobhi bhaji
Fried cabbage

Serves 4
Preparation time 25 minutes
Cooking time 35 minutes

A tasty side dish which can be eaten with puris, paraunthas or dall and rice.

METRIC/IMPERIAL	AMERICAN
100 g/4 oz ghee	$\frac{1}{2}$ cup ghee
1 small onion, chopped	1 small onion, chopped
6 cloves garlic, crushed	6 cloves garlic, crushed
1 teaspoon white cumin seeds	1 teaspoon white cumin seeds
1 teaspoon turmeric powder	1 teaspoon turmeric powder
1 medium white cabbage, coarsely chopped	1 medium head white cabbage coarsely chopped
100 g/4 oz potatoes, coarsely chopped	$\frac{1}{4}$ lb potatoes, coarsely chopped
100 g/4 oz shelled peas	$\frac{3}{4}$ cup shelled peas
100 g/4 oz carrots, sliced	$\frac{1}{4}$ lb carrots, sliced
salt to taste	salt to taste
225 g/8 oz tomatoes, peeled and sliced	$\frac{1}{2}$ lb tomatoes, peeled and sliced
1 teaspoon green mango powder	1 teaspoon green mango powder
1 green chilli, chopped	1 green chili, chopped
15 g/$\frac{1}{2}$ oz root ginger, grated	1 tablespoon grated root ginger
1 teaspoon garam masala	1 teaspoon garam masala
1 tablespoon chopped coriander leaves	1 tablespoon chopped coriander leaves
2 tablespoons melted butter	3 tablespoons melted butter

Melt the ghee in a saucepan and fry the onion and garlic with the cumin until golden brown. Add the turmeric and shake the pan for a few seconds.

Add the cabbage, potatoes, peas, carrots and salt. Cook, stirring continuously, for 5 minutes, then cover and cook over a low heat for 10 minutes.

Add the tomato, green mango powder, chilli and ginger. Stir well, replace the lid and continue to cook for a further 10 minutes.

Stir in the garam masala and coriander, heat through for 5 minutes then serve sprinkled with melted butter.

Rajvir arbi gapode
Yam foogath for the brave

Serves 4
Preparation time 20 minutes
Cooking time 40 minutes

Foogath is the name given to a dish which uses the leftovers of an already cooked vegetable or meat dish. In this way you can curry up the leftovers of the Sunday roast or the remains of a vegetable bhaji. There are three essential ingredients for a foogath; some cooked leftovers, coconut and mustard oil for frying. The recipe given below offers a new dimension to the range of teatime snacks and side dishes.

METRIC/IMPERIAL	AMERICAN
225 g/8 oz cooked yams	$\frac{1}{2}$ lb cooked yams
225 g/8 oz potatoes, parboiled	$\frac{1}{2}$ lb potatoes, parboiled
1 teaspoon salt	1 teaspoon salt
1 teaspoon mustard oil	1 teaspoon mustard oil
1 teaspoon mustard seeds	1 teaspoon mustard seeds
1 tablespoon chopped coriander leaves	1 tablespoon chopped coriander leaves
1 tablespoon grated coconut	1 tablespoon grated coconut
1 small onion, chopped	1 small onion, chopped
1 green chilli, chopped	1 green chili, chopped
1 teaspoon grated root ginger	1 teaspoon grated root ginger
oil for deep frying	oil for deep frying
Batter	*Batter*
3 tablespoons chick pea flour	$\frac{1}{4}$ cup chick pea flour
4 tablespoons water	$\frac{1}{3}$ cup water

Using a fork, mash the yams and potatoes together and add the salt.

Heat the oil in a frying pan and add the mustard seeds. Add the potato and yam mixture to the pan with the coriander, coconut, onion, chilli and ginger. Stir over a low heat for about 10 minutes. Remove the pan from the heat and allow the mixture to cool. Form the mixture into 12 small balls.

Heat the oil until a day-old cube of bread turns golden in 1 minute. Make a batter by mixing the chick pea flour with the water until smooth. Coat the balls in the batter and fry in the oil until light brown.

Serve with a chutney or sauce of your choice.

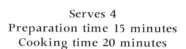

Baigan bhurta
Aubergine mash

Serves 4
Preparation time 15 minutes
Cooking time 20 minutes

Do not compare this to the sort of mashed potato dish found in the West. It is a lot more exotic, pungent and refreshingly different!

METRIC/IMPERIAL	AMERICAN
1 large aubergine	1 large eggplant
salt to taste	salt to taste
15 g/½ oz root ginger, grated	1 tablespoon grated root ginger
2 green chillies, chopped	2 green chilies, chopped
100 g/4 oz ghee	½ cup ghee
1 large onion, chopped	1 large onion, chopped
6 cloves garlic, crushed	6 cloves garlic, crushed
4 tablespoons chopped coriander leaves	⅓ cup chopped coriander leaves

Boil the aubergine in sufficient water to cover for 10-15 minutes. Allow to cool then remove the skin. Mash the aubergine flesh to a pulp and add the salt, ginger and chilli.

Heat the ghee in a frying pan and fry the onion and garlic until golden. Add the aubergine pulp and cook, stirring continuously, for 10-15 minutes. Serve sprinkled with the coriander as a dry dish.

Pichki arbi
Flattened artichokes

Serves 6
Preparation time 30 minutes
Cooking time 15 minutes

METRIC/IMPERIAL	AMERICAN
675 g/1½ lb Jerusalem artichokes	1½ lb Jerusalem artichokes
100 g/4 oz gram flour	1 cup gram flour
salt to taste	salt to taste
1 teaspoon red chilli powder	1 teaspoon red chili powder
1 tablespoon carom seeds	1 tablespoon carom seeds
1 green chilli, chopped	1 green chili, chopped
oil for deep frying	oil for deep frying

Boil the artichokes in water until tender, about 15 minutes then peel them.

Make a batter by gradually adding water to the gram flour to make a creamy mixture. Add salt to taste with the chilli powder, carom seeds and green chilli.

Heat the oil until a cube of day-old bread turns golden in 1 minute. Take each artichoke and flatten it between the palms. Dip them in the batter, one at a time and fry in the oil, two or three at a time. When golden brown, drain on absorbent kitchen paper and keep hot until all the artichokes are cooked. Serve hot or cold, as a dry dish with a meal or by themselves with a bread.

Bhindi bhaji
Fried okra

Serves 4
Preparation time 10 minutes
Cooking time 35 minutes

A delicious bhaji – eat it with paraunthas or rice and dall. Bhindis are also known as ladyfingers.

METRIC/IMPERIAL	AMERICAN
100 g/4 oz ghee or mustard oil	$\frac{1}{2}$ cup ghee or mustard oil
6 cloves garlic, crushed	6 cloves garlic, crushed
450 g/1 lb okra, sliced	1 lb ladyfingers, sliced
2 green chillies, chopped	2 green chilies, chopped
15 g/$\frac{1}{2}$ oz root ginger, grated	1 tablespoon grated root ginger
salt to taste	salt to taste
1 tablespoon green mango powder	1 tablespoon green mango powder
1 tablespoon butter	1 tablespoon butter
Spices	*Spices*
1 teaspoon turmeric powder	1 teaspoon turmeric powder
2 dry red chillies, crushed	2 dry red chilies, crushed
1 teaspoon white cumin seeds	1 teaspoon white cumin seeds

Heat the ghee or mustard oil in a frying pan and fry the garlic until light brown. Remove from the heat and add all the spices. Stir well and return to the heat. Now add the okra, chilli and ginger and mix well. Cook, uncovered, for 20 minutes, stirring occasionally.

When the okra is cooked, add the salt and green mango powder and cook for a further 5–10 minutes. Serve dotted with the butter.

Gobhi musallam
Whole cauliflower

Serves 4
Preparation time 20 minutes
Cooking time 1 hour

This dish can rightly claim to be the vegetarian cousin of the murgha (chicken) musallam.

METRIC/IMPERIAL	AMERICAN
8 cloves garlic, crushed	8 cloves garlic, crushed
15 g/½ oz root ginger, grated	1 tablespoon grated root ginger
salt to taste	salt to taste
2 tablespoons natural yogurt	3 tablespoons plain yogurt
1 medium cauliflower	1 medium head cauliflower
175 g/6 oz ghee	¾ cup ghee
2 medium onions, chopped	2 medium onions, chopped
2 bay leaves	2 bay leaves
6 tomatoes, peeled and sliced	6 tomatoes, peeled and sliced
juice of ½ lemon	juice of ½ lemon
150 ml/¼ pint water	⅔ cup water
Spices	*Spices*
½ teaspoon garam masala	½ teaspoon garam masala
1 brown cardamom	1 brown cardamom
8 black peppercorns	8 black peppercorns
4 cloves	4 cloves
1 teaspoon white cumin seeds	1 teaspoon white cumin seeds
1 teaspoon turmeric powder	1 teaspoon turmeric powder
Garnish	*Garnish*
1 teaspoon garam masala	1 teaspoon garam masala
1 green chilli, chopped	1 green chili, chopped
2 tablespoons chopped coriander leaves	3 tablespoons chopped coriander leaves

Mix together one-quarter of the garlic, 1 teaspoon of the ginger, the salt, yogurt and garam masala. Rub this paste all over the cauliflower.

Put the cauliflower into a covered pot or casserole and place that in a large saucepan with water to come halfway up the sides. Simmer the water for about 20 minutes so that the cauliflower is half-cooked by steam. Remove the cauliflower in the pot and set aside.

Heat the ghee in a saucepan and fry half the onion with the bay leaves, cardamom, peppercorns, cloves and cumin until golden brown. Add the turmeric and mix well.

Grind the remaining onion with the remaining garlic and ginger and add to the fried onion and spice mixture. Stir well and cook until the ghee starts to separate. Add the tomato, lemon juice and water and bring to the boil.

Pour this mixture over the cauliflower in the pot, cover and cook in a moderately hot oven (190°C, 375°F, Gas Mark 5) for 20 minutes, or until the cauliflower is completely cooked.

Sprinkle with garam masala, green chilli and coriander before serving.

Methi aloo bhaji
Fenugreek leaves and potatoes

Serves 4
Preparation time 20 minutes
Cooking time 30 minutes

This can be eaten with puris or paraunthas or served as a side dish with a main vegetarian meal.

METRIC/IMPERIAL	AMERICAN
4 tablespoons ghee or mustard oil	$\frac{1}{3}$ cup ghee or mustard oil
4 cloves garlic, crushed	4 cloves garlic, crushed
2 dry red chillies, crushed	2 dry red chilies, crushed
225 g/8 oz fenugreek leaves, chopped	$\frac{1}{2}$ lb fenugreek leaves, chopped
450 g/1 lb new potatoes, quartered	1 lb new potatoes, quartered
2 green chillies, chopped	2 green chilies, chopped
salt to taste	salt to taste

Heat the ghee or mustard oil in a frying pan and fry the garlic until golden. Add the red chillies and cook for a few seconds. Stir in the fenugreek, potato, green chilli and salt. Cook, stirring continuously, over a low heat for 2–3 minutes. Cover tightly and cook for 20 minutes, stirring occasionally. Serve hot.

Bharwan karele
Stuffed bitter gourds

Serves 4
Preparation time 20 minutes plus overnight marinating
Cooking time 50 minutes

The main problem with bitter gourds is their bitterness which must be removed before serving. As soon as you have mastered this art, you are in clover.

METRIC/IMPERIAL	AMERICAN
8 medium bitter gourds	8 medium bitter gourds
salt to taste	salt to taste
40 g/1½ oz tamarind	1½ oz tamarind
2 teaspoons green mango powder	2 teaspoons green mango powder
2 green chillies, finely chopped	2 green chilies, finely chopped
1 teaspoon sugar	1 teaspoon sugar
1 small and 2 large onions	1 small and 2 large onions
1 teaspoon lemon juice	1 teaspoon lemon juice
100 g/4 oz ghee	½ cup ghee
Spices	*Spices*
4 tablespoons coriander seeds	⅓ cup coriander seeds
2 tablespoons aniseeds	3 tablespoons anise seeds
1 tablespoon white cumin seeds	1 tablespoon white cumin seeds
1 tablespoon fenugreek seeds	1 tablespoon fenugreek seeds
1 teaspoon turmeric powder	1 teaspoon turmeric powder

Scrape the skin from the gourds and slit each one lengthways through the middle. Rub plenty of salt all over and inside the gourds and leave overnight. Wash the gourds under cold running water then boil with the tamarind in water to cover for 10–15 minutes. Rinse under cold running water and squeeze each gourd gently. Scoop some of the pulp out of each gourd.

Roast the first four spices together and grind to a powder. Add the turmeric, green mango powder, chilli, sugar and gourd pulp and mix well. Chop the small onion and mix into the stuffing, binding with the lemon juice. Divide the mixture into eight pieces and fill each gourd with a piece. Tie the gourds securely together with cotton to stop the stuffing escaping.

Heat the ghee in a frying pan and fry the gourds until light brown, turning them carefully. Drain and transfer to a plate to keep hot.

Slice the large onions lengthways and fry in the ghee left in the pan until just changing colour. Return the gourds to the pan and cook over a low heat for 10 minutes, turning frequently. Serve surrounded by the onions.

Bharwan baigan
Stuffed aubergines

Serves 6
Preparation time 30 minutes
Cooking time 20 minutes

This is another variety of stuffed vegetable. In Indian cuisine, minced meat is not generally used for stuffing aubergines.

METRIC/IMPERIAL	AMERICAN
6 aubergines	6 eggplants
2 green chillies, finely chopped	2 green chilies, finely chopped
1 teaspoon salt	1 teaspoon salt
2 tablespoons lemon juice	3 tablespoons lemon juice
100 g/4 oz ghee	$\frac{1}{2}$ cup ghee
1 large onion, finely chopped	1 large onion, finely chopped
Spices	*Spices*
4 tablespoons coriander seeds	$\frac{1}{3}$ cup coriander seeds
2 tablespoons aniseeds	3 tablespoons anise seeds
1 tablespoon white cumin seeds	1 tablespoon white cumin seeds
1 tablespoon fenugreek seeds	1 tablespoon fenugreek seeds
1 teaspoon turmeric powder	1 teaspoon turmeric powder

Clean the aubergines and slit them lengthways without halving them.

Roast the first four spices together then grind them to a powder and add the turmeric. Mix with the chilli, salt and lemon juice to make a stuffing. Divide this mixture between the aubergines and tie them back together with cotton to stop the stuffing escaping.

Heat the ghee in a large frying pan and fry the onion until light brown. Add the aubergines and cover tightly. Leave to cook turning occasionally until cooked, about 20–30 minutes.

Chaawal ki maze
Rice

Rice is the staple food of millions of people in India and is cooked into many different dishes. If possible buy the best quality Basmati, which has a flavour of its own. The best prepared rich dish, when cooked, shows each grain of rice separate, firm and fluffy and with no hard centre. The cooking of rice requires care and attention – it is not just a filler, it can be a real delicacy, fit for the finest feast anywhere in the world.

Rice can be cooked into fascinating and plush pullaos or moulded into romantic biriyanis. Sweet dishes are also created using rice, proving its versatility.

Saandaa chaawal
Plain boiled rice

Serves 4
Preparation time 35 minutes
Cooking time 25 minutes

Rice is eaten by about half the population of India. It is the staple diet of the South Indians, Bengalis and Biharis and is served with many vegetarian and meat meals.

METRIC/IMPERIAL	AMERICAN
225 g/8 oz long-grain rice	1 cup long-grain rice
600 ml/1 pint water	2½ cups water
2 tablespoons butter	3 tablespoons butter

Clean and wash the rice thoroughly and soak in water for about 30 minutes. Drain and discard the water.

Boil the measured water in a pan and add the rice. Half cover the pan and leave to boil for 10 minutes. When the grains are tender, drain off the water.

Return the pan to the heat, add the butter and mix thoroughly. Cover and leave over a very low heat for five minutes.

Serve hot with a variety of curries.

__Right__ Preparation for Stuffed herrings (see page 60).
__Overleaf__ Stuffed aubergines (see page 103); Prawn curry
(see page 69); Stuffed herrings (see page 60)

Khichdi
Boiled rice and dall mixture

Serves 4
Preparation time 45 minutes
Cooking time 20 minutes

*Khichdi is usually made of moong dall and is easily digested. There is
a saying in Hindi which says Khichdi has four boyfriends, namely,
Dahi, Papad, Ghee, and Achaar.*

METRIC/IMPERIAL	AMERICAN
100 g/4 oz dried black or green beans	$\frac{1}{2}$ cup dried black or green beans
100 g/4 oz long-grain rice	$\frac{1}{2}$ cup long-grain rice
600 ml/1 pint water	$2\frac{1}{2}$ cups water
1$\frac{1}{2}$ teaspoons salt	1$\frac{1}{2}$ teaspoons salt
100 g/4 oz ghee	$\frac{1}{2}$ cup ghee
1 green chilli, chopped	1 green chili, chopped
Spices	*Spices*
$\frac{1}{2}$ teaspoon turmeric powder	$\frac{1}{2}$ teaspoon turmeric powder
pinch of asafoetida powder	dash of asafoetida powder
1 teaspoon white cumin seeds	1 teaspoon white cumin seeds

Soak the beans and rice in water for 35–40 minutes. Drain, then add the
beans and rice with the salt and turmeric to the water. Cook over a moderate
heat for 15 minutes or until the water is absorbed and the rice and dall are
tender.

Heat the ghee in a frying pan and add the asafoetida powder, cumin and
green chilli. Leave the mixture over the heat for a few seconds and then add
to the pan with the dall mixture. Serve hot.

Left *Vegetable pasties (see page 123).*

Saandaa chaawal pullao
Plain rice pullao

Serves 4
Preparation time 25 minutes
Cooking time 25 minutes

This dish is also known as Kesaria pullao or saffron rice. It is a more sophisticated rice preparation, usually served with non-vegetarian meals, or on special occasions with vegetarian ones.

METRIC/IMPERIAL	AMERICAN
225 g/8 oz long-grain rice	1 cup long-grain rice
100 g/4 oz ghee	$\frac{1}{2}$ cup ghee
1 large onion, thinly sliced	1 large onion, thinly sliced
2 bay leaves	2 bay leaves
2 tomatoes, peeled and sliced	2 tomatoes, peeled and sliced
1 teaspoon salt	1 teaspoon salt
600 ml/1 pint water	$2\frac{1}{2}$ cups water
1 teaspoon hot water	1 teaspoon hot water
50 g/2 oz butter	$\frac{1}{4}$ cup butter
Spices	*Spices*
4 cloves	4 cloves
6 black peppercorns	6 black peppercorns
1 (2.5-cm/1-inch) piece cinnamon stick	1 (1-inch) piece cinnamon stick
1 brown cardamom	1 brown cardamom
$\frac{1}{2}$ teaspoon turmeric powder	$\frac{1}{2}$ teaspoon turmeric powder
pinch of saffron strands	dash of saffron strands

Wash and soak the rice in water for 20 minutes. Heat the ghee and fry half the onion with the bay leaves, cloves, peppercorns, cinnamon and cardamom until golden brown. Drain the rice and add to the ghee mixture with the turmeric and tomato. Stir thoroughly and add the salt gradually. Add the water, bring to the boil and leave over a low heat for 10 minutes, or until the water is absorbed and the rice is tender.

Steep the saffron in the hot water and sprinkle over the rice mixture.

Fry the remaining onion in the butter until crisp and brown and scatter over the rice pullao when serving.

Matar paneer pullao
Pea and cream cheese pullao

Serves 4
Preparation time 1 hour
Cooking time 35 minutes

This pullao has more flavour and class than a plain pullao. It is served as a special treat and goes rather well with a vegetarian meal.

METRIC/IMPERIAL	AMERICAN
450 g/1 lb long-grain rice	2 cups long-grain rice
175 g/6 oz ghee	¾ cup ghee
1 large onion, finely chopped	1 large onion, finely chopped
4 bay leaves	4 bay leaves
1 (113-g/4-oz) packet frozen peas	1 (4-oz) package frozen peas
1 medium potato, sliced	1 medium potato, sliced
225 g/8 oz paneer, (see page 22), cubed and fried	½ lb paneer, (see page 22), cubed and fried
1 green chilli, chopped	1 green chili, chopped
1½ teaspoons salt	1½ teaspoons salt
4 tomatoes, peeled and sliced	4 tomatoes, peeled and sliced
2 hard-boiled eggs, sliced	2 hard-cooked eggs, sliced
1 tablespoon chopped coriander leaves	1 tablespoon chopped coriander leaves
Spices	*Spices*
6 cloves	6 cloves
8 black peppercorns	8 black peppercorns
1 (5-cm/2-inch) piece cinnamon stick	1 (2-inch) piece cinnamon stick
4 green cardamoms, crushed	4 green cardamoms, crushed
1 brown cardamom	1 brown cardamom
1 teaspoon black cumin seeds	1 teaspoon black cumin seeds
½ teaspoon turmeric powder	½ teaspoon turmeric powder
1 teaspoon garam masala	1 teaspoon garam masala

Wash and soak the rice for 30 minutes then drain. Heat the ghee in a frying pan and add half the chopped onion, the bay leaves and the first six spices. Fry until golden. Add the turmeric, peas, potato, paneer and green chilli and fry for 10 minutes.

Boil the rice with the salt in water in a separate saucepan until half cooked. Drain and stir into the spice mixture. Add the garam masala and stir gently.

Arrange the tomato and egg slices on top of the rice and sprinkle with 2 teaspoons hot water and the coriander. Cover with a tightly fitting lid and leave over a low heat for 5–7 minutes or until the rice is fully cooked. Fry the remaining onion until golden and serve on the finished dish.

Gosht pullao
Mutton pullao

Serves 4
Preparation time 1 hour
Cooking time 2 hours

This is the basic pullao for non-vegetarian meals. You can use the meat of your choice for this dish. It is substantial and sustaining.

METRIC/IMPERIAL	AMERICAN
350 g/12 oz long-grain rice	1½ cups long-grain rice
225 g/8 oz meat	½ lb meat
175 g/6 oz ghee	¾ cup ghee
2 onions, chopped	2 onions, chopped
2 cloves garlic, crushed	2 cloves garlic, crushed
2 teaspoons salt	2 teaspoons salt
900 ml/1½ pints water	3¾ cups water
4 bay leaves	4 bay leaves
2 tablespoons natural yogurt	3 tablespoons plain yogurt
15 g/½ oz root ginger, crushed	1 tablespoon crushed root ginger
1 tablespoon tomato purée	1 tablespoon tomato paste
Spices	*Spices*
8 cloves	8 cloves
12 black peppercorns	12 black peppercorns
1 (5-cm/2-inch) piece cinnamon stick	1 (2-inch) piece cinnamon stick
1 brown cardamom	1 brown cardamom
4 green cardamoms	4 green cardamoms
1 teaspoon black cumin seeds	1 teaspoon black cumin seeds
1 teaspoon red chilli powder	1 teaspoon red chili powder
½ teaspoon ground cinnamon	½ teaspoon ground cinnamon

Soak the rice in water for 40 minutes, then drain. Cut the meat into 2.5-cm/1-inch cubes. Heat one-third of the ghee in a frying pan and fry half the onion and the garlic with 4 cloves, 8 black peppercorns, the cinnamon stick and brown cardamom until golden brown. Add the meat, stir and add 1 teaspoon of the salt and the water. Cover and cook over a low heat for about 1½ hours, or until the meat is tender. Drain the meat and reserve the stock.

Fry the remaining onion in the rest of the ghee with the bay leaves, 4 cloves, 4 black peppercorns and the green cardamoms. When the onion is golden, remove a small amount and reserve for the garnish.

Add the yogurt, ginger, tomato purée and remaining spices to the onion. Stir well, then add the soaked and drained rice and cooked meat to the mixture with the remaining salt. Gradually add the reserved stock and cook over a low heat for 15 minutes. Serve garnished with the reserved fried onions.

Jheenga pullao
Prawn pullao

Serves 4
Preparation time 45 minutes
Cooking time 30 minutes

This is a piscatorial delicacy that the Bengalis love to offer their guests. They would, of course, use mustard oil for frying. Whichever way you cook it, this pullao will leave a fragrant memory.

METRIC/IMPERIAL	AMERICAN
450 g/1 lb long-grain rice	2 cups long-grain rice
900 ml/1½ pints prawns, peeled	3¾ cups shrimp, shelled
oil for deep frying	oil for deep frying
100 g/4 oz ghee	½ cup ghee
1 large onion, finely chopped	1 large onion, finely chopped
4 bay leaves	4 bay leaves
1½ teaspoons salt	1½ teaspoons salt
2 tomatoes, peeled and sliced	2 tomatoes, peeled and sliced
900 ml/1½ pints water	3¾ cups water
100 g/4 oz cucumber, sliced	¼ lb cucumber, sliced
2 tablespoons butter, melted	3 tablespoons butter, melted
Paste	*Paste*
1 tablespoon coriander seeds, roasted	1 tablespoon coriander seeds, roasted
1 (2.5-cm/1-inch) piece root ginger, crushed	1 (1-inch) piece root ginger, crushed
1 medium onion, coarsely chopped	1 medium onion, coarsely chopped
6 cloves garlic, crushed	6 cloves garlic, crushed
Spices	*Spices*
4 cloves	4 cloves
8 black peppercorns	8 black peppercorns
4 green cardamoms	4 green cardamoms
2 (5-cm/2-inch) pieces cinnamon stick	2 (2-inch) pieces cinnamon stick
1 teaspoon black cumin seeds	1 teaspoon black cumin seeds
1 teaspoon garam masala	1 teaspoon garam masala

Clean, wash and soak the rice in water for 30 minutes. Wash the prawns and dry them thoroughly. Heat the oil until a day-old cube of bread turns brown in 1 minute. Fry the prawns until golden brown.

Heat the ghee in a saucepan and fry the large onion until crisp and brown. Remove half the fried onion and reserve for garnishing.

Add the bay leaves and the first five spices to the ghee and stir.

Grind all the paste ingredients together to make a smooth mixture. Add the paste to the ghee mixture and stir for 5 minutes. When the ghee begins to separate, add the prawns, salt and garam masala.

Drain the rice and add to the mixture with the tomato. Mix together and add the water. Leave the pan over a low heat for 10–15 minutes, or until the rice absorbs all the water.

Garnish with the reserved fried onions and arrange the cucumber slices around the edge of the serving dish. Sprinkle the pullao with melted butter before serving.

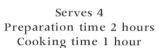

Goomaans biriyani
Beef biriyani

Serves 4
Preparation time 2 hours
Cooking time 1 hour

METRIC/IMPERIAL	AMERICAN
900 g/2 lb beef bones	2 lb beef bones
1.15 litres/2 pints water	5 cups water
225 g/8 oz chuck steak	$\frac{1}{2}$ lb chuck steak
225 g/8 oz ghee	1 cup ghee
1 large onion, chopped	1 large onion, chopped
2 tablespoons tomato purée	3 tablespoons tomato paste
350 g/12 oz long-grain rice	$1\frac{1}{2}$ cups long-grain rice
Paste	*Paste*
1 (2.5-cm/1-inch) piece root ginger, crushed	1 (1-inch) piece root ginger, crushed
4 cloves garlic, crushed	4 cloves garlic, crushed
1 small onion, grated	1 small onion, grated
4 tablespoons natural yogurt	$\frac{1}{3}$ cup plain yogurt
$1\frac{1}{2}$ teaspoons salt	$1\frac{1}{2}$ teaspoons salt
Spices	*Spices*
4 cloves	4 cloves
8 black peppercorns	8 black peppercorns
1 brown cardamom	1 brown cardamom
1 (5-cm/2-inch) piece cinnamon stick	1 (2-inch) piece cinnamon stick
$\frac{1}{2}$ teaspoon saffron strands	$\frac{1}{2}$ teaspoon saffron strands
Garnish	*Garnish*
2 tomatoes, peeled and sliced	2 tomatoes, peeled and sliced
1 green chilli, chopped	1 green chili, chopped
25 g/1 oz cashew nuts, fried and chopped	$\frac{1}{4}$ cup cashew nuts, fried and chopped
25 g/1 oz almonds, fried and chopped	$\frac{1}{4}$ cup almonds, fried and chopped

First make a stock by boiling the bones in the water with the first four spices for 1 hour.

Grind all the paste ingredients together to make a smooth mixture. Cut the meat into 2.5-cm/1-inch cubes, coat with the paste and leave for 30 minutes. Heat half the ghee and fry the meat over a low heat for about 15 minutes.

Heat the remaining ghee in a frying pan and fry the onion until golden brown. Remove a small amount and reserve for garnishing. Add the remaining onion to the fried meat with the tomato purée and stir well. Add the rice and fry with the meat for 5 minutes.

Add the stock to the onion mixture with half the saffron. Cook over a moderate heat for 15 minutes, or until the rice has absorbed all the liquid.

Put the rice mixture into a heated serving dish and garnish with the reserved fried onion. Steep the remaining saffron in a little hot water and sprinkle over the mixture.

Arrange the tomato around the edge of the dish and sprinkle with the chopped chilli and the fried nuts.

Murghi biriyani
Chicken biriyani

Serves 4
Preparation time 1 hour
Cooking time 50 minutes

This dish is superb and a gourmet's delight. If desired, duck can be substituted for chicken. Very wholesome and good for peace and quiet in the dining room!

METRIC/IMPERIAL	AMERICAN
8 chicken drumsticks	8 chicken drumsticks
175 g/6 oz ghee	$\frac{3}{4}$ cup ghee
25 g/1 oz almonds, chopped	$\frac{1}{4}$ cup almonds, chopped
25 g/1 oz cashew nuts, chopped	$\frac{1}{4}$ cup cashew nuts, chopped
1 large onion, finely chopped	1 large onion, finely chopped
4 bay leaves	4 bay leaves
450 g/1 lb long-grain rice	2 cups long-grain rice
900 ml/1$\frac{1}{2}$ pints warm water	3$\frac{3}{4}$ cups warm water
1 teaspoon salt	1 teaspoon salt
2 tablespoons butter, melted	3 tablespoons butter, melted
Paste	*Paste*
1 teaspoon garam masala	1 teaspoon garam masala
1 small onion, chopped	1 small onion, chopped
2 cloves garlic, crushed	2 cloves garlic, crushed
1 (5-cm/2-inch) piece root ginger	1 (2-inch) piece root ginger
1 (142-ml/5-fl oz) carton natural yogurt	1 (5-fl oz) carton plain yogurt
1 teaspoon salt	1 teaspoon salt
Spices	*Spices*
4 cloves	4 cloves
8 black peppercorns	8 black peppercorns
4 green cardamoms	4 green cardamoms
1 brown cardamom, crushed	1 brown cardamom, crushed
1 (5-cm/2-inch) piece cinnamon stick	1 (2-inch) piece cinnamon stick
$\frac{1}{2}$ teaspoon turmeric powder	$\frac{1}{2}$ teaspoon turmeric powder
$\frac{1}{2}$ teaspoon saffron strands	$\frac{1}{2}$ teaspoon saffron strands

Grind all the paste ingredients together to make a smooth mixture. Rub this over the chicken and leave for 30 minutes.

Heat the ghee in a frying pan and fry the almonds and cashews. Drain and reserve for garnish. In the ghee left in the pan fry the onion until golden and reserve half for garnish.

Add the bay leaves and first six spices to the remaining onion. Shake the pan and add the chicken. Cook for 20 minutes. Add the rice and mix well. Add the warm water and salt and leave over a moderate heat for 15–20 minutes until the water is absorbed and the rice is tender.

Steep the saffron in a little warm water, add the melted butter and stir into the rice mixture.

Garnish with the reserved fried onions and nuts.

Puri
Indian fried bread

Puris are small rounds of deep-fried bread, usually made from white flour. There are several varieties of puri, including kachoris, which are stuffed, and also some types of naan.

Khuskhusi puri
Crumbly deep fried bread

Serves 4
Preparation time 25 minutes
Cooking time 25 minutes

METRIC/IMPERIAL	AMERICAN
450 g/1 lb plain flour	4 cups all-purpose flour
pinch of salt	dash of salt
75 g/3 oz ghee or margarine	6 tablespoons ghee or margarine
oil for deep frying	oil for deep frying

Sift the flour and salt in a large basin. Add two-thirds of the ghee and rub in well. Make a well in the centre and gradually add enough water to make a stiff dough. Leave for 20 minutes. Knead the dough and divide into 16–18 portions. Dip each in the remaining ghee and flatten them out into 10-cm/4-inch diameter rounds.

Heat the oil in a deep frying pan until a day-old cube of bread turns golden in 1 minute. Fry each round for 10 seconds until golden on both sides. Drain on absorbent kitchen paper and put on a lined plate.

Dall kachori
Puri stuffed with dall

Serves 4
Preparation time 8½ hours
Cooking time 20 minutes

METRIC/IMPERIAL	AMERICAN
175 g/6 oz skinless dried black beans	¾ cup skinless dried black beans
450 g/1 lb plain flour	4 cups all-purpose flour
1 green chilli, chopped	1 green chili, chopped
½ teaspoon salt	½ teaspoon salt
oil for deep frying	oil for deep frying
Spices	*Spices*
1 tablespoon aniseeds	1 tablespoon anise seeds
1 teaspoon coriander seeds	1 teaspoon coriander seeds
½ teaspoon white cumin seeds	1 teaspoon white cumin seeds
½ teaspoon red chilli powder	½ teaspoon red chili powder
¼ teaspoon asafoetida powder	¼ teaspoon asafoetida powder

Soak the beans in water overnight then rinse and drain. Sift the flour into a basin and gradually add enough water to make a soft dough. Cover with a damp cloth and leave for 30 minutes.

Grind the drained beans with the chilli, salt and spices to make the stuffing. Mix well and divide into 16 portions.

Divide the dough into 16, using wet hands, and smear each portion with a little of the oil. Flatten and roll out into 5-cm/2-inch diameter rounds.

Wrap one portion of the stuffing in each round and roll into a smooth ball, using greased hands. Using a rolling pin, flatten each ball into a 7.5-cm/3-inch round.

Heat the oil in a deep frying pan until a cube of day-old bread turns golden in 1 minute. Fry one at a time, until golden on both sides.

Paneer kofte
Cream cheese kofta curry

Serves 6
Preparation time 30 minutes
Cooking time 1 hour

METRIC/IMPERIAL	AMERICAN
900 g/2 lb potatoes, quartered	2 lb potatoes, quartered
150 ml/¼ pint water	⅔ cup water
1 large green chilli, chopped	1 large green chili, chopped
1 teaspoon grated root ginger	1 teaspoon grated root ginger
salt to taste	salt to taste
2 tablespoons gram flour	3 tablespoons gram flour
2 tablespoons fresh breadcrumbs	3 tablespoons fresh soft bread crumbs
225 g/8 oz paneer (see page 22)	½ lb paneer (see page 22)
1 tablespoon grated coconut	1 tablespoon grated coconut
1 egg white, beaten	1 egg white, beaten
175 g/6 oz ghee	¾ cup ghee
2 bay leaves	2 bay leaves
2 medium onions, chopped	2 medium onions, chopped
6 cloves garlic, crushed	6 cloves garlic, crushed
1 (142-ml/5-fl oz) carton natural yogurt	1 (5-fl oz) carton plain yogurt
300 ml/½ pint water	1¼ cups water
Spices	*Spices*
½ teaspoon garam masala	½ teaspoon garam masala
1 tablespoon coriander seeds, roasted and ground	1 tablespoon coriander seeds, roasted and ground
4 cloves	4 cloves
1 brown cardamom	1 brown cardamom
6 black peppercorns	6 black peppercorns
1 teaspoon turmeric powder	1 teaspoon turmeric powder
1 teaspoon red chilli powder	1 teaspoon red chili powder
Topping	*Topping*
450 g/1 lb tomatoes, peeled and sliced	1 lb tomatoes, peeled and sliced
½ teaspoon garam masala	½ teaspoon garam masala
2 tablespoons chopped coriander leaves	3 tablespoons chopped coriander leaves

Boil the potatoes in the water with the green chilli, ginger and all but a pinch of the garam masala. When tender, drain and mash thoroughly with the salt, gram flour, breadcrumbs and coriander. Divide into 12 equal portions.

Mix the paneer with the coconut and remaining garam masala. Divide this into 12 equal portions. Flatten each portion of potato and use to wrap one portion of paneer. Roll into balls and brush with beaten egg white.

Heat the ghee and fry the balls until light brown all over. Drain and arrange in a casserole dish.

Add the bay leaves, onion, garlic, cloves, cardamom and peppercorns to the ghee left in the pan. Fry until the onion is golden brown. Add the yogurt and the turmeric and chilli powders. Mix well, pour in the water and bring to the boil. Simmer for 10 minutes.

Pour this sauce over the koftas, cover with the tomato, garam masala and coriander and cook in a moderate oven (180°C, 350°F, Gas Mark 4) for 10–15 minutes, or until heated through.

Andaa shorwedaar
Egg curry

Serves 4
Preparation time 30 minutes
Cooking time 40 minutes

METRIC/IMPERIAL	AMERICAN
100 g/4 oz ghee	$\frac{1}{2}$ cup ghee
8 eggs, hard-boiled	8 eggs, hard-cooked
1 large onion, finely chopped	1 large onion, finely chopped
2 bay leaves	2 bay leaves
4 cloves garlic, crushed	4 cloves garlic, crushed
1 teaspoon grated root ginger	1 teaspoon grated root ginger
2 tablespoons natural yogurt	3 tablespoons plain yogurt
4 large tomatoes, peeled and sliced	4 large tomatoes, peeled and sliced
1 teaspoon salt	1 teaspoon salt
300 ml/$\frac{1}{2}$ pint hot water	1$\frac{1}{4}$ cups hot water
Spices	*Spices*
2 cloves	2 cloves
1 (5-cm/2-inch) piece cinnamon stick	1 (2-inch) piece cinnamon stick
1 brown cardamom	1 brown cardamom
5 black peppercorns	5 black peppercorns
$\frac{1}{2}$ teaspoon black cumin seeds	$\frac{1}{2}$ teaspoon black cumin seeds
1 teaspoon turmeric powder	1 teaspoon turmeric powder
1 teaspoon red chilli powder	1 teaspoon red chili powder
1 tablespoon coriander seeds, roasted and ground	1 tablespoon coriander seeds, roasted and ground
Garnish	*Garnish*
1 tablespoon garam masala	1 tablespoon garam masala
2 tablespoons chopped coriander leaves	2 tablespoons chopped coriander leaves

Heat the ghee in a frying pan and fry the shelled eggs until light brown. Drain the eggs and set aside.

Fry the onion in the ghee left in the pan together with the bay leaves, cloves, cinnamon stick, cardamom, peppercorns and cumin. Fry until the onion is golden brown. Remove from the heat and add the turmeric, chilli and coriander powders, garlic, ginger and yogurt and mix well. Return to the heat and cook for 2 minutes. Add the tomato and salt and cook, stirring, for 10 minutes.

Stir in the water and bring to the boil. Add the eggs and simmer for 10 minutes. Garnish with the garam masala and coriander.

Golgappa or Puchka
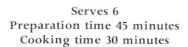
Hollow crispy wafers

Serves 6
Preparation time 45 minutes
Cooking time 30 minutes

This is an ideal low-calorie savoury dish for weight-watchers, and of course others, too! Served with the spiced water and chick peas together with the blend of exotic spices, these delicate wafers have a flavour quite unique! One could eat dozens of them without feeling guilty.
Though you can keep the golgappas and water separately for long periods, the two together (zeera jal in golgappa) should not be kept for more than a few seconds, or they will become soggy and messy.

METRIC/IMPERIAL	AMERICAN
225 g/8 oz flour	2 cups flour
100 g/4 oz semolina	$\frac{2}{3}$ cup semolina
50 g/2 oz urad dall flour	$\frac{1}{2}$ cup urad dall flour
2 teaspoons ghee, melted	2 teaspoons ghee, melted
water to bind	water to bind
oil for deep frying	oil for deep frying
2 tablespoons cooked or canned chick peas	3 tablespoons cooked or canned chick peas
To serve	*To serve*
salt	salt
red chilli powder	red chili powder

Mix the flour, semolina and dall flour with the ghee and knead, gradually adding the minimum of water to make a stiff dough. Cover with a damp cloth and leave for about 30 minutes. Knead again for a couple of minutes and divide the dough into four portions. Roll each portion into a ball and then, applying a little of the oil and greasing the surface, roll out into as large and thin a round as possible. Now take a sharp-edged bottle top, about 3 cm/1½ inches in diameter, and cut out small rounds. Roll these out again to smooth their edges. Keep covered with a damp cloth.

Heat the oil in a deep pan until a day-old cube of bread turns golden in 1 minute. Slide in four rounds at a time. They are cooked when they are golden brown on both sides and are puffed up. To help the discs puff up, make slight waves in the oil by holding a ladle perpendicularly in the middle of the pan and gently shaking it. Lower the heat from time to time so that the oil does not become too hot.

When the golgappas are cooked, drain them on absorbent kitchen paper and allow to cool. Take one and make a hole in the top with your finger. Fill with chick peas and put it into your mouth, all in one piece. If required, you may add further salt or chilli powder on top of each helping.

Andaa kachoomar
Egg mishmash

Serves 4
Preparation time 10 minutes
Cooking time 10 minutes

This dish is so quick to make it's ideal for a lazy bachelor. If you are starving and have no time to prepare elaborate dishes, eat this with bread and Indian pickles.

METRIC/IMPERIAL	AMERICAN
6 eggs	6 eggs
1 medium onion, chopped	1 medium onion, chopped
1 teaspoon grated root ginger	1 teaspoon grated root ginger
2 green chillies, chopped	2 green chilies, chopped
salt to taste	salt to taste
$\frac{1}{2}$ teaspoon freshly ground black pepper	$\frac{1}{2}$ teaspoon freshly ground black pepper
100 g/4 oz ghee	$\frac{1}{2}$ cup ghee
2 tomatoes, peeled and sliced	2 tomatoes, peeled and sliced
1 tablespoon chopped coriander leaves to garnish	1 tablespoon chopped coriander leaves to garnish

Beat the eggs together in a bowl for 2 minutes. Mix in the onion, ginger, chilli, salt and pepper.

Heat the ghee in a frying pan and pour in the egg mixture. Fry, stirring continuously over a moderate heat for about 3–5 minutes, or until the egg thickens and sets. Add the tomato and mix well. Serve sprinkled with coriander.

Keema samosa
Minced meat pasty

Serves 6
Preparation time 1 hour
Cooking time 30 minutes

This dish is a snack which can be eaten hot or cold. It is good served at parties, with drinks, for tea or picnics. The dish is popular throughout the continent of Asia and, I suspect, beyond!

METRIC/IMPERIAL	AMERICAN
2 tablespoons milk	3 tablespoons milk
oil for deep frying	oil for deep frying
sauce or chutney to serve	sauce or chutney to serve
Pastry	*Pastry*
450 g/1 lb plain flour	4 cups all-purpose flour
1 teaspoon salt	1 teaspoon salt
175 g/6 oz margarine	$\frac{3}{4}$ cup margarine
150 ml/$\frac{1}{4}$ pint water	$\frac{2}{3}$ cup water
Filling	*Filling*
1 tablespoon butter	1 tablespoon butter
1 small onion, chopped	1 small onion, chopped
$\frac{1}{2}$ teaspoon white cumin seeds	$\frac{1}{2}$ teaspoon white cumin seeds
225 g/8 oz minced meat	$\frac{1}{2}$ lb ground meat
1 green chilli, finely chopped	1 green chili, finely chopped
1 teaspoon salt	1 teaspoon salt
100 g/4 oz cooked peas	$\frac{3}{4}$ cup cooked peas
pinch of freshly ground black pepper	dash of freshly ground black pepper
1 teaspoon chopped coriander leaves	1 teaspoon chopped coriander leaves

To make the pastry, sift the flour and salt into a large bowl. Warm the margarine so that it is soft and add it to the flour, rubbing it in until the mixture resembles fine breadcrumbs. Stir in the water, a little at a time, and knead until a hard dough is formed. Cover the dough with a damp cloth and leave for about 15 minutes.

To make the filling, melt the butter in a saucepan and add the onion and cumin seeds. Stir over a moderate heat for 5–7 minutes. Add the mince, chilli and salt and mix thoroughly. Lower the heat and cook for a further 10 minutes, stirring occasionally.

Add the peas and stir in. Leave over a moderate heat for 5 minutes or until all the liquid has evaporated. Remove the pan from the heat, add the pepper and coriander and mix thoroughly. Allow to cool before use.

Divide the dough into 12 equal portions. Roll each one out to a thin 18-cm/7-inch diameter round. Cut each round through the middle using a sharp kitchen knife. Cover these semi-circles with a damp cloth while you are filling them, one at a time.

Take one semi-circle and brush the edges with milk. With the semi-circle on a flat surface, spoon some cooled filling into the centre and fold in the corners, overlapping them to form a cone. Add more filling if required then fold over and seal the top to make a triangle. Repeat the process with all the other semi-circles to use up all the filling. Cover the samosas not being fried, with a damp cloth, keeping them separated from each other.

Heat the oil in a deep pan until a day-old cube of bread turns golden in 1 minute. Slide four samosas at a time into the oil. Lower the heat a little and fry until the samosas are light brown on both sides. Take care when turning them over that the filling does not escape.

When cooked, remove from the pan and drain on absorbent kitchen paper. Serve hot with sauce or chutney of your choice.

Aloo samosa
Vegetable pasty

Serves 6
Preparation time 1 hour
Cooking time 30 minutes

These pasties are cooked in exactly the same way as the keema samosas, but they have a vegetarian filling. Use the same pastry as for the previous recipe and form and fill the pasties in just the same way.

METRIC/IMPERIAL	AMERICAN
1 tablespoon ghee	1 tablespoon ghee
pinch of asafoetida powder	dash of asafoetida powder
2 teaspoons mustard seeds	2 teaspoons mustard seeds
450 g/1 lb potatoes, parboiled and diced	1 lb potatoes, parboiled and diced
100 g/4 oz cooked peas	$\frac{3}{4}$ cup cooked peas
2 green chillies, chopped	2 green chilies, chopped
1½ teaspoons salt	1½ teaspoons salt
1 teaspoon pomegranate seeds	1 teaspoon pomegranate seeds
1 teaspoon garam masala	1 teaspoon garam masala
2 tablespoons chopped coriander leaves	3 tablespoons chopped coriander leaves

Heat the ghee in a frying pan and add the asafoetida powder, mustard seeds, potato, peas, chilli, salt and pomegranate seeds. Stir well over a moderate heat for about 2 minutes. Cover the pan, lower the heat and leave to cook for about 10 minutes. Add the garam masala and coriander and stir well. Allow this filling to cool before use.

Kadhi
Gram flour fritters in yogurt

Serves 6
Preparation time 25 minutes
Cooking time 1 hour

This is a dish enjoyed by vegetarians and meat eaters alike!

METRIC/IMPERIAL	AMERICAN
225 g/8 oz gram flour	2 cups gram flour
$\frac{1}{2}$ teaspoon baking powder	$\frac{1}{2}$ teaspoon baking powder
oil for deep frying	oil for deep frying
2 (142-ml/5-fl oz) cartons natural yogurt	2 (5-fl oz) cartons plain yogurt
300 ml/$\frac{1}{2}$ pint buttermilk	1$\frac{1}{4}$ cups buttermilk
2 tablespoons ghee	3 tablespoons ghee
1 green chilli, chopped	1 green chili, chopped
salt to taste	salt to taste
Spices	*Spices*
1 tablespoon mustard or fenugreek seeds	1 tablespoon mustard or fenugreek seeds
pinch of asafoetida powder	dash of asafoetida powder
$\frac{1}{2}$ teaspoon turmeric powder	$\frac{1}{2}$ teaspoon turmeric powder
Garnish	*Garnish*
100 g/4 oz ghee	$\frac{1}{2}$ cup ghee
$\frac{1}{2}$ teaspoon red chilli powder	$\frac{1}{2}$ teaspoon red chili powder

Sift the gram flour into a basin and gradually add enough water to make a thick batter. Beat in the baking powder and leave to stand for 15 minutes.

Heat the oil until a day-old cube of bread turns golden in 1 minute then drop teaspoonfuls of the batter into the oil, keeping them separate. Cook 10–12 at a time, draining the cooked ones on absorbent kitchen paper. You should end up with 20–25 fritters.

Mix together the yogurt, buttermilk and any leftover batter.

Heat the ghee in a saucepan, add the mustard or fenugreek and asafoetida powder. Shake the pan for a few seconds. Add the green chilli and turmeric then stir in the yogurt mixture. Add salt to taste and simmer for 15 minutes.

Drop the fritters into the mixture and simmer over a moderate heat for about 15 minutes.

Melt the ghee for garnishing in a frying pan and add the chilli powder. Pour this over the yogurt dish and serve with boiled rice or chapatis.

Right *Leavened baked bread (see page 133); Pappadums (see page 130); Layered parauntha (see page 134); Puris (see page 116); Chapati (see page 131).*
Overleaf *Chicken biriyani (see page 115); Cocktail curry (see page 91).*

Navratan pakode
Cocktail fritters

Serves 6
Preparation time 15 minutes
Cooking time 20 minutes

An admirable accompaniment for tea or drinks. You can ring the changes by using different vegetables.

METRIC/IMPERIAL	AMERICAN
450 g/1 lb gram flour	4 cups gram flour
450 ml/$\frac{1}{4}$ pint water	2 cups water
$\frac{1}{2}$ teaspoon bicarbonate of soda	$\frac{1}{2}$ teaspoon baking soda
4 green chillies, finely chopped	4 green chilies, finely chopped
1 medium onion, chopped	1 medium onion, chopped
$\frac{1}{2}$ cauliflower, cut into florets	$\frac{1}{2}$ head cauliflower, cut into florets
1 medium potato, diced	1 medium potato, diced
100 g/4 oz peas, fresh or frozen	$\frac{3}{4}$ cup peas, fresh or frozen
oil for deep frying	oil for deep frying

Make a thick batter by whisking together the gram flour and water. Make sure that there are no lumps. Add the next six ingredients to the batter and mix well. Leave to stand for about 10 minutes.

Heat the oil in a deep pan until a day-old cube of bread turns golden in 1 minute. Drop 1 tablespoon of the vegetable batter into the oil, being careful not to splash. Make several drops like this at a time. Fry these fritters until they are golden brown all over. Repeat with all the remaining batter. Drain the cooked fritters on absorbent kitchen paper.

Left *Boiled rice and dall mixture (see page 109); Egg curry (see page 119).*

Roti
Indian breads

The Indian breads are well known throughout the world and are in a class by themselves. The most popular among the breads is the chapati. *It is a flat round pancake of wholemeal flour dough which is cooked on a griddle. To eat a well cooked chapati is truly a pleasurable experience.*
Naan *is another bread that goes down extremely well with meat dishes. Although traditionally the naan should be cooked in a clay oven (tandoor) it can also be cooked under a grill or on direct heat, without losing the authentic taste.*
A parauntha *is a griddle-cooked bread which, unlike a chapati, is cooked with a little ghee or oil on the griddle.*

Papad
Savoury wafers or pappadums

Serves 6
Preparation time 5 minutes
Cooking time 5 minutes

Papads are a well known savoury side dish which add elegance and style to a meal. There are distinct differences between them – the ones sold in the Bengal and Maharashtra are thick and fluffy and rather bland, those in south India are paper thin and very crisp. In Uttar Pradesh and the Delhi regions, they are flavoured with asafoetida and are studded with crushed black pepper and red chilli powder. Papad making is a trade in India and people hand down the skill for generations to obtain perfect results.

METRIC/IMPERIAL	AMERICAN
oil for frying	oil for frying
12 papads, halved if required	12 papads, halved if required

Two-thirds fill a medium saucepan with oil and heat to near smoking point. Put a small piece of papad in the pan to see if the temperature of the oil is right. If it sizzles immediately, the oil is ready for frying. Lower the heat and drop one papad in the pan. Press it down with a ladle to save it from curling up. It will sizzle and spread out to its full size, about 15 cm/6 inches in diameter. Turn it over and cook for 3–4 seconds on the other side. Remove the papad from the pan and stand it edgeways on absorbent kitchen paper so that the excess fat is drained off. If not fully crisp, place the papad under a hot grill for a few seconds before serving.
Serve fresh and hot, by itself or with vegetarian or non-vegetarian meals.

Phulke or Tawe ki roti
Chapati

Serves 6
Preparation time 45 minutes
Cooking time 20 minutes

An essential dish on the vegetarian menu. A chapati is wholesome and sustaining – it is not generally eaten by itself, but makes a meal complete when eaten with a dall, curry or meat dish.

METRIC/IMPERIAL	AMERICAN
675 g/1½ lb wholemeal flour	6 cups whole meal flour
4 tablespoons plain flour	⅓ cup all-purpose flour
ghee or butter for serving	ghee or butter for serving

Turn the wholemeal flour into a bowl and gradually mix in enough water to make a pliable dough. Leave to rest for 30 minutes. Knead again then pull off pieces about the size of ping-pong balls. Dip these in the plain flour and flatten them out, using a rolling pin. This should make 12–15 chapatis.

Heat a griddle or heavy-bottomed frying pan until very hot, then cook each chapati for 15–20 seconds on each side, turning it when brown spots appear underneath. Press lightly all over, using a clean cloth, and the chapati will puff up. Repeat the process with each chapati.

Serve the chapatis soon after cooking with plenty of butter to accompany any curry, dall or dry dish. Wrap them in a clean cloth to keep them hot and soft.

Makke ki roti
Cornflour chapati

Serves 4
Preparation time 30 minutes
Cooking time 30 minutes

The typical cornflour chapati is thick and large, with a lot of ghee spread over the surface. Slow cooking adds to its flavour. These are excellent served with a dall or curry.

METRIC/IMPERIAL	AMERICAN
450 g/1 lb cornflour	4 cups cornstarch
2 tablespoons ghee	3 tablespoons ghee

Sift the cornflour into a basin and gradually add enough water to make a pliable dough. Knead the dough for about 20 minutes. Leave covered with a damp cloth for 10 minutes. Knead for a further 5 minutes and divide the dough into eight portions.

Flatten each portion, using damp hands, to make rounds. Cover the rounds which are not being cooked with a damp cloth. Heat a griddle or heavy-bottomed frying pan and brush with a little ghee. Cook each chapati on the griddle then under the grill. The chapatis are cooked when brown spots appear on both sides. Serve hot with ghee.

Besan ki roti
Gram flour chapatis

Serves 4
Preparation time 15 minutes
Cooking time 15 minutes

The gram flour adds flavour and texture to the chapatis. They are heavier on the stomach than the plain variety but are very delicious. Particularly good served with vegetarian meals.

METRIC/IMPERIAL	AMERICAN
225 g/8 oz wholemeal flour	2 cups whole meal flour
225 g/8 oz gram flour	2 cups gram flour
butter or ghee for serving	butter or ghee for serving

Mix the flours together and gradually add enough water to make a pliable dough. Divide into ten portions and flatten them out using a rolling pin.

Heat a griddle or heavy-bottomed frying pan until very hot, and cook the chapatis for about 30 seconds on each side. Keep pressing the sides with a clean cloth until brown spots appear underneath.

Butter the chapatis generously and serve with lentils, vegetables or curries.

Naan
Leavened baked bread

Serves 6
Preparation time 4½ hours
Cooking time 30 minutes

This great dish comes from the Punjab and goes very well with the tandoori meat dishes as well as vindaloos. Traditionally, naans are baked in clay ovens, but the method given here should suit everybody. They must be eaten fresh and hot, so serve them as you cook them.

METRIC/IMPERIAL	AMERICAN
350 g/12 oz plain flour	3 cups all-purpose flour
1½ teaspoons sugar	1½ teaspoons sugar
1 teaspoon salt	1 teaspoon salt
½ teaspoon baking powder	½ teaspoon baking powder
15 g/½ oz fresh yeast	1 teaspoon compressed yeast
150 ml/¼ pint warm milk	⅔ cup warm milk
1 (142-ml/5-fl oz) carton natural yogurt	1 (5-fl oz) carton plain yogurt
100 g/4 oz butter	½ cup butter
2 tablespoons poppy seeds	3 tablespoons poppy seeds

Sift the flour into a large bowl and stir in the sugar, salt and baking powder. Dissolve the yeast in the milk and stir in the yogurt. Mix thoroughly with the flour to form a dough. Knead until smooth then cover and leave to rise in a warm place for about 4 hours.

Divide the risen dough into 12 equal portions and roll into balls. On a lightly floured surface, flatten the balls into oblong shapes, using both hands and slapping the naan from one hand to another.

Lightly grease and heat a griddle or heavy-bottomed frying pan until very hot. Cook the naan on one side only. Spread the raw side with butter and poppy seeds and transfer to a hot grill. Cook until browned and serve hot.

Parati parauntha
Layered parauntha

Serves 6
Preparation time 40 minutes
Cooking time 25 minutes

This is a superior type of parauntha – more filling and tastier than the basic version. They can be eaten with virtually any vegetable or meat dish. Some people eat them for breakfast with yogurt. I'm sure you will like them.

METRIC/IMPERIAL	AMERICAN
675 g/1½ lb chapati flour	6 cups chapati flour
50 g/2 oz margarine	¼ cup margarine
225 g/8 oz ghee	1 cup ghee

Sift the flour into a bowl and rub in the margarine. Gradually add enough warm water to make a smooth, pliable dough. Leave to rest for 30 minutes, then divide into 18 portions.

Roll each portion into a ball, flatten each one on a floured surface into a 10-cm/4-inch diameter round. Spread ¼ teaspoon ghee on the surface of each round then fold in half, keeping the ghee inside. Repeat the process to achieve a triangular shape. When all the pieces have been rolled and folded, roll them out on a floured surface to 15 cm/6 inches on each side.

Heat a griddle or heavy-bottomed frying pan and spread 1 teaspoon ghee over the surface. Cook each parauntha for 30 seconds on each side, re-greasing the griddle between each turn. Cook the first side again to make sure it is cooked. Dark brown spots should appear on the surface. Serve hot.

Mooli parauntha
Parauntha stuffed with radish

Serves 6
Preparation time 40 minutes
Cooking time 20 minutes

A different variety of parauntha which can be eaten on its own if liked – scrumptious and very satisfying. Eat them with potato curry, papad, yogurt or pickles.

METRIC/IMPERIAL	AMERICAN
450 g/1 lb chapati flour	4 cups chapati flour
225 g/8 oz white radish, grated	$\frac{1}{2}$ lb white radish, grated
100 g/4 oz onions, chopped	$\frac{1}{4}$ lb onions, chopped
2 green chillies, finely chopped	2 green chilies, finely chopped
$\frac{1}{2}$ teaspoon salt	$\frac{1}{2}$ teaspoon salt
$\frac{1}{2}$ teaspoon grated root ginger	$\frac{1}{2}$ teaspoon grated root ginger
225 g/8 oz ghee	1 cup ghee

Sift the flour and gradually add enough water to form a smooth dough. Cover with a damp cloth and leave for 20 minutes. Squeeze the water from the radish and mix the grated flesh with the onion, chilli, salt and ginger. Mix this stuffing thoroughly.

Divide the dough into 12 equal pieces. Using a rolling pin on a floured surface, flatten each piece into a 10-cm/4-inch diameter round. Take 1 tablespoon of the stuffing, place in the middle of a round and enclose it completely, folding the edges of the dough in to make a ball. Roll the ball flat on a floured surface to a 15-cm/6-inch round.

Heat a griddle or heavy-bottomed frying pan until very hot, spread 1 tablespoon of ghee over the surface and place the parauntha on top. Cook for 15 seconds, then turn. Spread 1 teaspoon ghee over the griddle and cook the parauntha for 20 seconds. Turn over again. Brown spots should appear on both sides when it is cooked. Turn as often as necessary until the parauntha is cooked. Serve hot.

Keema parauntha
Minced meat parauntha

Serves 4
Preparation time 40 minutes
Cooking time 30 minutes

*This delectable delicacy is intended for the fastidious guest who prefers
a non-vegetarian bread. It is a meal in itself, but eat it with whatever
you fancy.*

METRIC/IMPERIAL	AMERICAN
350 g/12 oz chapati flour	3 cups chapati flour
175 g/6 oz ghee	¾ cup ghee
Stuffing	*Stuffing*
225 g/8 oz minced meat	½ lb ground meat
250 ml/8 fl oz water	1 cup water
1 small onion, finely chopped	1 small onion, finely chopped
2 green chillies, chopped	2 green chilies, chopped
1 teaspoon grated root ginger	1 teaspoon grated root ginger
¼ teaspoon freshly ground black pepper	¼ teaspoon freshly ground black pepper
2 cloves garlic, crushed	2 cloves garlic, crushed
½ teaspoon garam masala	½ teaspoon garam masala

Sift the flour into a basin and gradually add enough water to make a smooth
dough. Knead thoroughly.

Divide the dough into eight equal portions and leave for 30 minutes.

Mix all the stuffing ingredients together in a saucepan and cook until the
water has evaporated and the meat is cooked.

Flatten each piece of dough on a floured board to a 7.5-cm/3-inch diameter
round, using a rolling pin. Put one-eighth of the stuffing on each round then
fold the dough over to enclose the stuffing, forming a ball. Roll the balls out
to 13-cm/5-inch diameter rounds.

Heat a griddle or heavy-bottomed frying pan and spread 1 teaspoon ghee
over the surface. Cook the paraunthas one at a time on it for 30 seconds on
each side. Grease the griddle again then cook the second side for 30 seconds,
Re-cook the first side for 20 seconds and the second side for 20–25 seconds,
greasing the griddle between turns. Brown spots should show when the
paraunthas are cooked. Serve hot.

Chatni
Chutneys and sauces

Chutneys are essential for perking up a meal. Most of them are made by grinding the ingredients together but some are made just by chopping and mixing a few ingredients together. There are also other specialist chutneys or sauces which entail a little more preparation. I have included a few of these such as zeera jal and chilli vinegar.

Sirka
Chilli vinegar

Preparation time 10 weeks
Storage time 1 year

This vinegar is made from the juice of sugarcanes. Instead of a pickle or chutney, serve vinegar with sliced onion, salt and pepper. Vinegar is also used in pickles. For a milder vinegar, add a little sugar.

METRIC/IMPERIAL	AMERICAN
2.24 litres sugarcane juice	10 cups sugarcane juice
1 tablespoon salt	1 tablespoon salt
10 red chillies	10 red chilies

Pour the sugarcane juice into a strong china or earthenware pot. Cover with a clean cloth and leave in a well lit and warm place for 8 weeks. It is best left in the sun during the day. A thick layer will form on top and this will begin to ferment.

After 8 weeks, strain the juice through a muslin or fine sieve twice. Add the salt and chillies and leave in a warm place for 2 weeks.

Pour the fermented vinegar into dry sterilised jars or bottles. Seal and use as required.

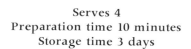

Karonda chatni
Gooseberry chutney

Serves 4
Preparation time 10 minutes
Storage time 3 days

This accompaniment is a popular way of adding pungency and piquancy to a vegetarian meal.

METRIC/IMPERIAL	AMERICAN
225 g/8 oz gooseberries	$\frac{1}{2}$ lb gooseberries
1$\frac{1}{2}$ teaspoons salt	1$\frac{1}{2}$ teaspoons salt
1 medium green chilli, chopped	1 medium green chili, chopped
1 tablespoon chopped mint	1 tablespoon chopped mint

Top and tail the gooseberries, cut in half and remove the seeds. Grind the flesh with all the other ingredients to make a paste. Serve as a side dish.

Tamatar chatni
Tomato chutney

Serves 4
Preparation time 15 minutes
Storage time 2 days

Most chutneys are best eaten fresh, this is no exception but you can store any leftover chutney in the refrigerator for 2 days.

METRIC/IMPERIAL	AMERICAN
2 medium tomatoes, peeled and crushed	2 medium tomatoes, peeled and crushed
4 small spring onions, chopped	4 small scallions, chopped
1 small green chilli, chopped	1 small green chili, chopped
small piece root ginger, finely chopped	small piece root ginger, finely chopped
$\frac{1}{2}$ teaspoon salt	$\frac{1}{2}$ teaspoon salt
pinch of freshly ground black pepper	dash of freshly ground black pepper
1 teaspoon chopped coriander leaves	1 teaspoon chopped coriander leaves
1 tablespoon lemon juice	1 tablespoon lemon juice

Mix all the ingredients together thoroughly. Serve, using a wooden or stainless spoon, with any meal.

Aam chatni
Mango chutney

Serves 4
Preparation time 10 minutes
Storage time 3 days

METRIC/IMPERIAL
100 g/4 oz green mango, sliced
1 medium green chilli, chopped
1 teaspoon salt
2 tablespoons chopped mint

AMERICAN
$\frac{1}{4}$ lb green mango, sliced
1 medium green chili, chopped
1 teaspoon salt
3 tablespoons chopped mint

Grind all the ingredients together, using a pestle and mortar, to form a thick pulp. Serve as a side dish. For a sweet and sour effect add $1-1\frac{1}{2}$ teaspoons sugar.

Chatpati chatni
Green chillies and root ginger in lemon juice

Serves 4
Preparation time 8 minutes
Storage time 2 days

METRIC/IMPERIAL
225 g/8 oz onions, chopped
50 g/2 oz root ginger, grated
2 green chillies, coarsely chopped
2 tablespoons chopped coriander
leaves
$\frac{1}{2}$ teaspoon freshly ground black
pepper
1 teaspoon salt
juice of 1 lemon
6 red radishes, sliced

AMERICAN
$\frac{1}{2}$ lb onions, chopped
$\frac{1}{3}$ cup grated root ginger
2 green chilies, coarsely chopped
3 tablespoons chopped coriander
leaves
$\frac{1}{2}$ teaspoon freshly ground black
pepper
1 teaspoon salt
juice of 1 lemon
6 red radishes, sliced

Mix together all the ingredients and serve as a side dish.

Zeera jal or Puchka pani
Spiced water

Preparation time 55 minutes
Storage time 2 days

A great appetiser! It can be drunk by itself – with crushed ice, or used
for filling golgappas or puchkas, the famous chaat dish.

METRIC/IMPERIAL	AMERICAN
225 g/8 oz seedless tamarind pulp	½ lb seedless tamarind pulp
900 ml/1½ pints warm water	3¾ cups warm water
3 tablespoons salt	¼ cup salt
1 teaspoon black salt	1 teaspoon black salt
2 teaspoons sugar	2 teaspoons sugar
2 large dry red chillies	2 large dry red chilies
1 teaspoon grated root ginger	1 teaspoon grated root ginger
1 tablespoon chopped mint or 1 teaspoon mint sauce	1 tablespoon chopped mint or 1 teaspoon mint sauce
1 tablespoon lemon juice	1 tablespoon lemon juice
Spices	*Spices*
pinch of asafoetida powder	dash of asafoetida powder
2 teaspoons white cumin seeds	2 teaspoons white cumin seeds
2 teaspoons coriander seeds	2 teaspoons coriander seeds
2 teaspoons aniseeds	2 teaspoons anise seeds
½ teaspoon carom seeds	½ teaspoon carom seeds
15 black peppercorns	15 black peppercorns

Soak the tamarind in one-third of the warm water for 30 minutes. Rub the pulp through a sieve into a jug. Discard any husk left in the sieve. Add the rest of the water to the tamarind.

  Roast all the spices together then grind with the next six ingredients, leaving the lemon juice, to make a paste. Gradually stir the spice paste into the tamarind mixture, shaking the jug and mixing after each addition. Add the lemon juice and refrigerate until required. Stir well before serving.

Sonth
Sweet sauce

Preparation time 2½ hours
Storage time 4 days

METRIC/IMPERIAL

100 g/4 oz seedless tamarind pulp
175 g/6 oz jaggery (palm sugar)
300 ml/½ pint warm water
1 teaspoon ghee
50 g/2 oz dried dates, chopped and soaked
25 g/1 oz sultanas, soaked
1½ teaspoons salt
1 tablespoon chopped mint or 1 teaspoon mint sauce
Spices
2 teaspoons ground ginger
1 teaspoon white cumin seeds
½ teaspoon asafoetida powder
1 teaspoon red chilli powder
1 teaspoon aniseeds, roasted and ground

AMERICAN

¼ lb seedless tamarind pulp
¾ cup jaggery (palm sugar)
1¼ cups warm water
1 teaspoon ghee
½ cup chopped dried dates, soaked
3 tablespoons seedless white raisins
1½ teaspoons salt
1 tablespoon chopped mint or 1 teaspoon mint sauce
Spices
2 teaspoons ground ginger
1 teaspoon white cumin seeds
½ teaspoon asafoetida powder
1 teaspoon red chili powder
1 teaspoon anise seeds, roasted and ground

Soak the tamarind and jaggery together in the water for 1½ hours. Mash the mixture thoroughly and press it through a sieve. Discard the husk. Mix the ginger into the pulp and set aside.

Heat the ghee in a frying pan and fry the cumin and asafoetida powder together. Mix in the tamarind pulp and sauté lightly. Add the dates, sultanas, salt and chilli and aniseed powders and mix thoroughly. Bring to the boil then remove from the heat and allow to cool. Add the mint leaves when the mixture is cold and store in the refrigerator until it is required.

Raita
Whisked yogurt dishes

Yogurt (see page 22) is very versatile and plays an important role in the preparation of many Indian dishes. Apart from being instrumental in the making of some delicious curries and having some marinating possibilities, the most notable contribution yogurt makes to Indian cuisine is the raita dish. Raita is the name given to a yogurt-based savoury preparation served as a side dish.

Kheera raita
Cucumber raita

Serves 4
Preparation time 10 minutes

This is the best known raita in the West. While in India it is an inexpensive and popular dish, it is regarded as something of a delicacy in the West. It tastes great anywhere!

METRIC/IMPERIAL	AMERICAN
1 (142-ml/5-fl oz) carton natural yogurt	1 (5-fl oz) carton plain yogurt
salt to taste	salt to taste
$\frac{1}{4}$ teaspoon freshly ground black pepper	$\frac{1}{4}$ teaspoon freshly ground black pepper
1 tablespoon chopped mint	1 tablespoon chopped mint
100 g/4 oz cucumber, peeled and grated	$\frac{1}{4}$ lb cucumber, peeled and grated
1 green chilli, chopped	1 green chili, chopped
$\frac{1}{4}$ teaspoon red chilli powder	$\frac{1}{4}$ teaspoon red chili powder
1 teaspoon ground cumin seeds	1 teaspoon ground cumin seeds

Beat the yogurt with a fork for 2–3 minutes then stir in the salt, pepper, mint, cucumber and green chilli. Mix well and turn into a serving dish. Sprinkle with chilli powder and cumin.

Boondi raita
Batter drop raita

Serves 4
Preparation time 45 minutes

A truly fantastic side dish! It is my favourite and I'm sure it will be
yours too. Serve it with vegetarian or non-vegetarian meals.

METRIC/IMPERIAL

2 (142-ml/5-fl oz) cartons natural
yogurt
$\frac{1}{2}$ teaspoon black salt
$\frac{1}{2}$ teaspoon salt
$\frac{1}{4}$ teaspoon freshly ground black
pepper
$1\frac{1}{2}$ teaspoons white cumin seeds,
roasted and ground
100 g/4 oz boondi (see page 23)
1 teaspoon red chilli powder
1 green chilli, chopped
1 tablespoon chopped mint,
coriander leaves or parsley

AMERICAN

2 (5-fl oz) cartons plain yogurt
$\frac{1}{2}$ teaspoon black salt
$\frac{1}{2}$ teaspoon salt
$\frac{1}{4}$ teaspoon freshly ground black
pepper
$1\frac{1}{2}$ teaspoons white cumin seeds,
roasted and ground
1 cup boondi (see page 23)
1 teaspoon red chili powder
1 green chili, chopped
1 tablespoon chopped mint,
coriander leaves or parsley

Beat the yogurt with a fork for 2–3 minutes and add the salts, pepper and half
the cumin. Soak the boondi in warm water for 20–30 minutes.

Squeeze the water from the boondi using a muslin cloth. Drop the boondi
into the yogurt and mix thoroughly. Serve topped with chilli powder, green
chilli, chosen chopped leaves and the remaining cumin.

Baigan raita
Aubergine raita

Serves 4
Preparation time 15 minutes

A rather unusual dish in the world of raitas. If you like aubergines, you will love it. If liked, another vegetable suitably prepared, such as marrow or potato, can be substituted.

METRIC/IMPERIAL	AMERICAN
2 long aubergines	2 long eggplant
225 g/8 oz ghee	1 cup ghee
2 (142-ml/5-fl oz) cartons natural yogurt	2 (5-fl oz) cartons plain yogurt
1 teaspoon salt	1 teaspoon salt
1 teaspoon white cumin seeds, roasted and ground	1 teaspoon white cumin seeds, roasted and ground
1 tablespoon chopped mint	1 tablespoon chopped mint
1 green chilli, chopped	1 green chili, chopped
$\frac{1}{2}$ teaspoon red chilli powder	$\frac{1}{2}$ teaspoon red chili powder

Slice the aubergines and heat the ghee in a frying pan. Fry the slices until golden brown then set aside. Beat the yogurt with the salt, cumin, mint and green chilli. Soak the aubergine in the yogurt and serve sprinkled with the chilli powder.

Right *Preparation for Tomato chutney (see page 138); Mango chutney (see page 139); Green chillies and root ginger in lemon juice (see page 139).*
Overleaf *Yogurt (see page 22); Batter drop raita (see page 143); Batter drops (see page 23); Tomato chutney (see page 138); Mango chutney (see page 139); Green chillies and root ginger in lemon juice (139).*

Achar
Pickles

Pickles perk up a meal; giving a contrast of flavour and taste. They boost the appetite generally and some of them stimulate digestion. They go particularly well with bland foods such as the dalls and plain boiled rice. Like wine, pickles will acquire more taste, colour and maturity with time and will become that much more delicious.

Aam ka meetha achar
Mango sweet pickle

Preparation time 30 minutes
Pickling time 7 days
Storage time 15 days

If you like a sweet pickle, this one is the last word.

METRIC/IMPERIAL	AMERICAN
675 g/1½ lb green mangoes	1½ lb green mangoes
575 g/1¼ lb sugar	2½ cups sugar
2 teaspoons salt	2 teaspoons salt
Spices	*Spices*
1 tablespoon white cumin seeds	1 tablespoon white cumin seeds
2 teaspoons brown cardamom seeds	2 teaspoons brown cardamom seeds
1 tablespoon poppy seeds	1 tablespoon poppy seeds
1 teaspoon red chilli powder	1 teaspoon red chili powder

Wash, peel and grate the mangoes. There should be about 450 g/1 lb of flesh. Add the sugar and salt and mix well in a large bowl.

Roast the first three spices together, stir in the chilli powder and mix with the sweetened mango.

Turn the pickle into a sterilised jar, cover with a clean cloth and leave out in the sun or in a warm, light place for about 1 week. Shake the jar at least once a day.

Left *Apple preserve (see page 153); Carrot preserve (see page 152).*

Neebu sirka achar
Lemon pickle in vinegar

Preparation time 30 minutes
Pickling time 10 to 15 days
Storage time 2 months

This is a beautiful tangy pickle which can be eaten with any main meal. It aids digestion and is particularly palatable with less spicy dishes.

METRIC/IMPERIAL	AMERICAN
35 lemons	35 lemons
1.15 litres/2 pints water	5 cups water
1 teaspoon asafoetida powder	1 teaspoon asafoetida powder
4 teaspoons salt	4 teaspoons salt
Paste	*Paste*
30 black peppercorns	30 black peppercorns
2 teaspoons brown cardamom seeds	2 teaspoons brown cardamom seeds
2 tablespoons salt	3 tablespoons salt
2 teaspoons red chilli powder	2 teaspoons red chili powder
1 tablespoon white cumin seeds	1 tablespoon white cumin seeds
15 cloves	15 cloves
2 tablespoons sugar	3 tablespoons sugar
2 tablespoons vinegar	3 tablespoons vinegar

Wash and clean the lemons. Now boil the water and put 25 lemons in it for 2–3 minutes. Take them out, dry them and cut into quarters.

Using sterilised jars for the pickle, sprinkle the asafoetida powder and half the salt over the base. Grind all the paste ingredients to make a smooth mixture and smear it all over the lemon quarters. Drop these spiced lemon pieces into the jars. Squeeze the juice from the remaining lemons over them and sprinkle with the rest of the salt.

Cover the jars with clean cloths and leave out in the sun or a well lit and warm place. The pickle should be ready in about 2 weeks.

Mirch khatta achar
Chilli pickle in lemon juice

Preparation time 30 minutes
Pickling time 1 day
Storage time 7 days

You will like this pickle, even if you are not a great chilli fan. The lemon juice does wonders for it, and it can be made very quickly.

METRIC/IMPERIAL	AMERICAN
10 chillies	10 chilies
2 teaspoons salt	2 teaspoons salt
5 tablespoons lemon juice	6 tablespoons lemon juice
Spices	*Spices*
large pinch asafoetida powder	large dash asafoetida powder
4 teaspoons mustard seeds	4 teaspoons mustard seeds
1 teaspoon fenugreek seeds	1 teaspoon fenugreek seeds
2 teaspoons white cumin seeds	2 teaspoons white cumin seeds

Split the chillies down the middle. Roast the spices and grind them together. Add the salt to the spices and stuff this mixture into the chillies. Place the chillies in a sterilised glass jar, pour the lemon juice over them and put the jar outside in the sun or a well lit and warm place for a day. Shake the jar, or bottle in which the pickle is stored before serving.

NOTE If a warm place is not available, the lemon juice can be heated up a little before it is poured over the chillies.

Murabba
Preserves

*Preserves unlike sweetmeats, can sometimes be stored for up to a year;
store them in sterilised jars and use them as you wish.*

Gajar ka murabba
Carrot preserve

**Preparation time 45 minutes
Cooking time 25 minutes
Storage time 1 week**

*This delicacy is said to be good for the brain and has cooling
properties. It is usually served cold.*

METRIC/IMPERIAL	AMERICAN
900 g/2 lb carrots	2 lb carrots
900 g/2 lb sugar	4 cups sugar
600 ml/1 pint water	$2\frac{1}{2}$ cups water
juice of 1 lemon	juice of 1 lemon
$\frac{1}{2}$ teaspoon cardamom seeds, coarsely ground	$\frac{1}{2}$ teaspoon cardamom seeds, coarsely ground

Peel the carrots and discard the woody part. Cut the flesh into large pieces
and prick all over with a fork. Put the pieces in a saucepan with enough
water to cover and bring to the boil. As soon as the water has boiled, remove
from the heat and drain off all the water.

Prepare a one-string syrup by dissolving the sugar in the water (see page
26). Boil gently. Add the carrot to the syrup and stir in the lemon juice.
Continue cooking over a low heat until the carrot is tender and the syrup is
thick. Allow to cool then stir in the cardamom before serving.

Seb ka murabba
Apple preserve

Preparation time 45 minutes
Cooking time 25 minutes
Storage time 5 days

A great favourite with the intellectual fraternity, this preserve has a delicious flavour and is said to have soothing properties.

METRIC/IMPERIAL	AMERICAN
675 g/1½ lb medium cooking apples	1½ lb medium baking apples
2 teaspoons eating lime powder	2 teaspoons eating lime powder
1.15 litres/2 pints water	5 cups water
900 g/2 lb sugar	4 cups sugar
600 ml/1 pint water	2½ cups water
2 tablespoons rose water	3 tablespoons rose water
pieces of gold foil	pieces of gold foil

Wash the apples and slice the tops and bottoms off, then prick the whole apples all over, using a fork. Mix the eating lime and water and soak the apples in this mixture for 30 minutes. Rinse the apples in cold running water several times and dry them completely.

Make a one-string syrup by dissolving the sugar in the water over a low heat (see page 26). Boil the syrup gently and add the apples. Continue cooking until the syrup is thick and the apples are completely cooked. Remove from the pan and allow to cool.

Serve each apple with a little syrup and rose water. Cover each apple with a piece of foil. Store the apples in an airtight container.

Mithian
Indian sweetmeats

Indian sweetmeats offer outstanding food value. Most of them are made from either milk, khoya or chhena (see pages 29 and 22) or a combination of these.
Because of their milk base, further strengthened by the addition of the nuts and flavourings, the sweetmeats are rich and sustaining.
Pahalwans (wrestlers) and other muscle men often thrive on a regular diet of malai pedas, burfi and bucketfuls of milk, which give them strength and energy.
The mention of success in some event or celebration of an occasion in India invariably sparks off a demand for sweetmeats and guests are offered them as a sign of welcome and hospitality.

Gulab jamun
Cream cheese balls in syrup

Serves 6
Preparation time 30 minutes
Cooking time 30 minutes

This universally liked dish is soft and syrupy and tastes gorgeous!

METRIC/IMPERIAL	AMERICAN
225 g/8 oz khoya (see page 29)	$\frac{1}{2}$ lb khoya (see page 29)
25 g/1 oz flour	$\frac{1}{4}$ cup flour
40 g/1$\frac{1}{2}$ oz paneer (see page 22)	3 tablespoons paneer (see page 22)
12 small pieces sugar candy	12 small pieces sugar candy
450 g/1 lb sugar	2 cups sugar
300 ml/$\frac{1}{2}$ pint water	1$\frac{1}{4}$ cups water
225 g/8 oz ghee	1 cup ghee
2 tablespoons rose water	3 tablespoons rose water

Mix the khoya, flour and paneer together and form the mixture into 12 small balls. Wrap a piece of sugar candy in each piece of the mixture.

Make a one-string syrup by dissolving the sugar in the water (see page 26). Boil the syrup gently until the required stage is reached.

Heat the ghee in a saucepan until a day-old cube of bread turns golden in 1 minute. Fry the balls until golden all over. Drain the balls on absorbent kitchen paper then immerse them in the syrup. Leave for about 10 minutes before eating. Sprinkle with rose water before serving.

Jalebi
Batter coils in syrup

Serves 4
Preparation time 2 hours
Cooking time 20 minutes

Jalebis are the youngsters' finger-licking favourites. They are easy to make and are very refreshing first thing in the morning. The secret of this sweet is that they should be eaten soon after being made, when they are crisp and hot, otherwise they become soft and unappetising.

METRIC/IMPERIAL	AMERICAN
175 g/6 oz plain flour	1½ cups all-purpose flour
50 g/2 oz gram flour, lightly fried	½ cup gram flour, lightly fried
4 tablespoons natural yogurt	⅓ cup plain yogurt
7 g/¼ oz fresh yeast	½ cake compressed yeast
300 ml/½ pint water	1¼ cups water
225 g/8 oz sugar	1 cup sugar
½ teaspoon saffron powder	½ teaspoon saffron powder
½ teaspoon green cardamom seeds, ground	½ teaspoon green cardamom seeds, ground
oil for deep frying	oil for deep frying

Mix the flours with the yogurt, yeast and water to form a thick creamy batter. Set aside for about 2 hours to ferment. Whisk thoroughly before use.

Prepare a one-string syrup by dissolving the sugar in the water over a low heat (see page 26). Boil gently. Just before the syrup is ready, add the saffron and cardamom powders.

Heat the oil until a cube of day-old bread turns golden in 1 minute. Pour the batter through a baster in a steady stream (or coconut shell with a hole) into the pan to form coils. Make a few at a time. Deep fry these for about 30 seconds then turn them to ensure that they are golden and crisp all over but are not brown.

Remove from the pan, drain on absorbent kitchen paper and immerse in the prepared syrup. Leave for 3–4 minutes so that they can soak up as much syrup as possible.

Take them out of the syrup, and serve hot.

Petha
Whitegourd sweetmeat

Serves 6
Preparation time 8 hours
Cooking time 35 minutes

*This dish is a famous offering from Agra the city renowned for the
Taj Mahal. Eat it with syrup or dry – for the latter version, continue
cooking until the sugar granulates.*

METRIC/IMPERIAL	AMERICAN
450 g/1 lb whitegourd flesh	1 lb whitegourd flesh
1 teaspoon eating lime powder	1 teaspoon eating lime powder
450 ml/¾ pint water	2 cups water
575 g/1¼ lb sugar	2½ cups sugar
6 pieces silver foil	6 pieces silver foil
2 tablespoons rose water	3 tablespoons rose water

Cut the whitegourd flesh into cubes and prick them all over with a fork. Mix
the eating lime with sufficient water to cover all the cubes in a large pan.
Leave overnight or for 8 hours. Drain the cubes and rinse several times in
cold running water.

  Prepare a one-string syrup by dissolving the sugar in the water over a low
heat (see page 26). Lower the drained cubes into the boiling syrup and cook
over a moderate heat for about 20 minutes. Check the syrup from time to time
to see that it is not getting too thick. When the syrup has completely soaked
into the cubes, remove from the heat and leave to cool.

  Cover the cubes with the foil and serve with the rose water sprinkled on
top.

Malai peda
Milk sweetmeat

Serves 6
Preparation time 5 minutes
Cooking time 40 minutes

METRIC/IMPERIAL	AMERICAN
900 ml/1½ pints milk	3¾ cups milk
75 g/3 oz sugar	6 tablespoons sugar
pinch of citric acid, mixed with 2 tablespoons water	dash of citric acid, mixed with 3 tablespoons water
½ teaspoon saffron strands	½ teaspoon saffron strands
1 teaspoon cornflour	1 teaspoon cornstarch
½ teaspoon green cardamom seeds, ground	½ teaspoon green cardamom seeds, ground
1 teaspoon pistachios, flaked	1 teaspoon pistachios, flaked
1 teaspoon flaked almonds	1 teaspoon flaked almonds

Boil the milk until it is reduced to half. Add the sugar and boil again for about 5 minutes. Now add the citric acid mixture gradually, until the milk curdles a little (you may not need to use more than half of this mixture). Then add the saffron and cornflour to the boiling milk.

Lower the heat and go on cooking, stirring continuously until the mixture leaves the side of the pan clean. Add the cardamom powder and mix well. Then cool before handling it.

Take small pieces from the dough and shape them into short fat rounds. Decorate them with the pistachio and almond flakes, put them into sweet papers and serve.

NOTE The leftover sweetmeats can be stored in a cool place for later use, but do not use a refrigerator.

Nariyal burfi
Coconut toffee

Serves 6
Preparation time 40 minutes
Cooking time 15 minutes

METRIC/IMPERIAL
225 g/8 oz coconut, fresh or dry,
ground
225 g/8 oz khoya (see page 29)
1 tablespoon ghee
1 teaspoon cardamom seeds, coarsely
ground
575 g/1¼ lb sugar
450 ml/¾ pint water
½ tablespoon grated pistachios
½ tablespoon grated almonds

AMERICAN
½ lb coconut, fresh or dry, ground
½ lb khoya (see page 29)
1 tablespoon ghee
1 teaspoon cardamom seeds, coarsely
ground
2½ cups sugar
2 cups water
½ tablespoon grated pistachios
½ tablespoon grated almonds

Mix the coconut and khoya together and then fry lightly in the ghee over a low heat. Add the ground cardamom and mix thoroughly. Prepare a one-string syrup by dissolving the sugar in the water over a low heat (see page 26). Boil gently. Stir the coconut mixture into the syrup.

  Grease a large plate and sprinkle the grated nuts on it. Now spread the khoya mixture evenly over the plate and let it cool. With the help of a kitchen knife, cut it into the desired shapes – squares, diamonds or whatever. Turn them over so that the nut covered part appears on the top and serve cold.

Jaipur paag
Gram flour diamonds

Serves 6
Preparation time 5 minutes
Cooking time 30 minutes

This is a sweetmeat for all seasons, but do not let young children eat too many of them as they are very sweet.

METRIC/IMPERIAL
3 tablespoons water
175 g/6 oz sugar
100 g/4 oz gram flour
225 g/8 oz ghee
1 teaspoon flaked almonds
1 teaspoon chopped pistachios

AMERICAN
¼ cup water
¾ cup sugar
1 cup gram flour
1 cup ghee
1 teaspoon flaked almonds
1 teaspoon chopped pistachios

Heat the water over a moderate heat in a large pan and then dissolve the sugar in it. Now add the gram flour and keep stirring to dissolve any lumps.

Heat the ghee in a separate pan and keep on one side.

When the gram flour mixture begins to bubble, add the hot ghee a little at a time. Keep stirring continuously, keeping the heat at moderate. The mixture will thicken as it cooks. Eventually it will become bubbly and like a honeycomb. At this point remove the pan from the heat.

Spread evenly on a greased plate and cut into diamond shapes while still warm.

Sprinkle the nuts on the top and serve warm or cold.

Besan laddu
Chick pea flour rounds

Serves 6
Preparation time 5 minutes
Cooking time 20 minutes

Laddus are great balls of nourishing fun, to eat before, during or after meals. There are many varieties of this dish, but besan laddus are my particular favourites.

METRIC/IMPERIAL	AMERICAN
225 g/8 oz ghee	1 cup ghee
225 g/8 oz chick pea flour	2 cups chick pea flour
350 g/12 oz castor sugar	1½ cups sugar
Nuts	*Nuts*
1 teaspoon chopped cashew nuts	1 teaspoon chopped cashew nuts
1 teaspoon chopped almonds	1 teaspoon chopped almonds
1 teaspoon chopped pistachios	1 teaspoon chopped pistachios

Place the ghee and chick pea flour in a pan over a low heat. Keep stirring to avoid the formation of lumps. When it is cooked, it will release an appetising and aromatic smell. Remove the pan from the heat and let it cool.

Add the sugar and nuts to the chick pea mixture and stir in thoroughly. Now mould the mixture into small balls of the required size. You now have laddus to serve hot or cold.

Shanti sandesh
Message of peace discs

Serves 4
Preparation time 10 minutes
Cooking time 30 minutes

This sweetmeat is especially liked by students and those engaged in intellectual work. They sell by the billion in India during the examination period.

METRIC/IMPERIAL
150 g/5 oz sugar
225 g/8 oz paneer (see page 22)
1 tablespoon rose water
$\frac{1}{2}$ teaspoon green cardamom seeds,
coarsely ground
10 pistachios, thinly sliced and
crushed

AMERICAN
$\frac{2}{3}$ cup sugar
$\frac{1}{2}$ lb paneer (see page 22)
1 tablespoon rose water
$\frac{1}{2}$ teaspoon green cardamom seeds,
coarsely ground
10 pistachios, thinly sliced and
crushed

Mix together the sugar and the paneer. Put the mixture in a pan and place it over a low heat. Stir it quickly and continuously in order to avoid the formation of lumps. When the mixture solidifies, splash the rose water on it and remove the pan from the heat. Stir a few more times.

Place the pistachio and cardamom crumbs on two separate plates and put to one side.

Now divide the mixture into several portions of the required size and flatten them to give the desired shapes. Dip each portion into both plates in turn so that the front of the sandesh is coated with crumbs. Serve cold.

Suji halwa
Semolina sweet

Serves 6
Preparation time 10 minutes
Cooking time 20 minutes

This dish is a standard offering at all the Sikh religious gatherings. It is a light food for the breakfast table and is universally popular.

METRIC/IMPERIAL	AMERICAN
175 g/6 oz ghee	$\frac{3}{4}$ cup ghee
175 g/6 oz fine semolina	1 cup fine semolina
150 ml/$\frac{1}{4}$ pint water	$\frac{2}{3}$ cup water
50 g/2 oz seedless raisins, soaked	$\frac{1}{3}$ cup seeded raisins, soaked
25 g/1 oz desiccated coconut (optional)	$\frac{1}{3}$ cup shredded coconut (optional)
25 g/1 oz almonds, shredded	$\frac{1}{4}$ cup almonds, shredded
1 teaspoon green cardamom seeds, ground	1 teaspoon green cardamom seeds, ground
100 g/4 oz sugar	$\frac{1}{2}$ cup sugar

Melt the ghee over a low heat in a frying pan. Add the semolina and fry for about 10 minutes, stirring continuously. Now add the water, raisins, coconut (if used) and half each of the almonds and cardamom powder. When the water is fully absorbed, add the sugar. Keep stirring until the ingredients are well mixed.

Remove from the heat, sprinkle with the rest of the almonds and the cardamom and serve hot.

Kheers
Puddings

Kheers have their own exalted place in the annals of Indian cookery. They are rich dishes and are cooked and eaten on special occasions by the various sections of the community. Kheers in India are often decorated with pounded thin silver or gold papers (warq) which are digestible and very attractive

Nariyal kheer
Coconut pudding

Serves 4
Preparation time 5 minutes
Cooking time 45 minutes

I am sure this superb pudding will be a hit with all in your family after its very first appearance. The coconut, the dry fruits and the rose water all lend this dish a distinctive Indian flavour.

METRIC/IMPERIAL	AMERICAN
75 g/3 oz sugar	6 tablespoons sugar
900 ml/1½ pints creamy milk	3¾ cups creamy milk
50 g/2 oz ghee	¼ cup ghee
100 g/4 oz coconut, fresh or dry, grated	¼ lb coconut, fresh or dry, grated
1 teaspoon green cardamom seeds	1 teaspoon green cardamom seeds
½ teaspoon saffron strands	½ teaspoon saffron strands
2 tablespoons rose water	3 tablespoons rose water
Dry fruits	*Dry fruits*
25 g/1 oz sultanas	3 tablespoons seedless white raisins
25 g/1 oz flaked almonds	¼ cup flaked almonds
25 g/1 oz pistachios, chopped	¼ cup pistachios, chopped
15 g/½ oz whole chironji	3 tablespoons whole chironji

Pour the sugar and milk into a saucepan and bring to the boil gradually. Remove the pan from the heat after the second boiling and put to one side.

In another pan heat the ghee and the grated coconut and fry over a low heat until golden. Now add the milk from the other pan and leave it to thicken over a low heat, stirring continuously. When the milk is reduced to half, add all the dry fruits and cardamom and leave for a further 5 minutes.

Remove from the heat and serve when cool. Sprinkle with a few sprigs of saffron and generous quantities of rose water.

Makhana kheer
Makhana pudding

Serves 6
Preparation time 10 minutes
Cooking time 1¼ hours

This is a most exotic Indian pudding, with a taste to match. Eaten hot or cold, it is a gourmet's delight.

METRIC/IMPERIAL	AMERICAN
100 g/4 oz selected soft white makhanas	¼ lb selected soft white makhanas
1 teaspoon ghee	1 teaspoon ghee
1.15 litres/2 pints creamy milk	5 cups creamy milk
4 tablespoons sugar	⅓ cup sugar
1 tablespoon shredded almonds	1 tablespoon shredded almonds
1 tablespoon grated pistachios	1 tablespoon grated pistachios
1 teaspoon green cardamom seeds, ground	1 teaspoon green cardamom seeds, ground

Halve the makhanas and place in a saucepan with the ghee. Fry over a low heat for about 5 minutes. Add the milk and sugar and stir well. Leave to simmer for about 1 hour, until the milk is reduced to half and assumes a creamy consistency. During this period, stir from time to time in order to ensure that the milk does not boil over or stick to the bottom of the pan. Now add the almonds and pistachios and leave for a further 10 minutes. Sprinkle with the ground cardamom and serve hot.

NOTE This dish can also be served cold, in which case leave it in the refrigerator for about 30 minutes and serve with a sprinkling of rose water.

Kela, santara kheer

Banana and satsuma pudding

Serves 4
Preparation time 15 minutes
Making time 5 minutes

METRIC/IMPERIAL	AMERICAN
2 teaspoons sugar	2 teaspoons sugar
½ teaspoon freshly ground black pepper	½ teaspoon freshly ground black pepper
½ teaspoon red chilli powder	½ teaspoon red chili powder
1 teaspoon salt	1 teaspoon salt
2 (142-ml/5-fl oz) cartons natural yogurt	2 (5-fl oz) cartons plain yogurt
2 large bananas, peeled and thinly sliced	2 large bananas, peeled and thinly sliced
2 large satsumas, peeled in segments with pips removed	2 large satsumas, peeled in segments with pips removed
½ teaspoon saffron strands	½ teaspoon saffron strands

Mix the sugar, pepper, chilli powder, salt and yogurt together. Add the bananas and satsumas and mix together for about 2 minutes.

Steep the saffron in a teaspoon of water and sprinkle it over the dish before serving.

Rabri

Fresh dried milk

Serves 4
Preparation time 5 minutes
Cooking time 2 hours

METRIC/IMPERIAL	AMERICAN
2.25 litres/4 pints creamy milk	10 cups creamy milk
4 tablespoons sugar	⅓ cup sugar
4 green cardamom seeds	4 green cardamom seeds
4 drops of kewra essence	4 drops of kewra extract
pinch of green cardamom powder	dash of green cardamom powder
pinch of pistachio powder	dash of pistachio powder

Bring the milk to the boil in a deep, heavy-bottomed non-stick pan. Add the sugar and cardamom seeds and leave to simmer over a low heat for 2 hours until the milk is reduced to about one quarter. Remove from the heat and add the kewra essence.

Sprinkle with the cardamom and pistachio powders and serve hot or cold with faluda (see page 169).

Faluda
Cold vermicelli

Serves 4
Preparation time 5 minutes
Cooking time 30 minutes

Faluda is a collective name for the transparent semi-solid shapes of a jelly-like consistency, made from arrowroot. These can be eaten by themselves, with just a spoonful of sugar syrup and a few drops of rose water. Faluda invariably accompanies the kulfi dish.

METRIC/IMPERIAL	AMERICAN
450 g/1 lb arrowroot	4 cups arrowroot
1.15 litres/2 pints water	5 cups water

Mix the arrowroot and water in a saucepan and bring to the boil, stirring continuously. Cook over a low heat until a thick paste is formed.

Stand the faluda machine (a hand-mincer fitted with a perforated disc) over a bucket of cold water. Push the paste through the machine and large vermicelli strands will fall into the bucket. When all the faluda is made, change the water a few times.

Keep the faluda in the cold fresh water and serve directly from there, without any water as far as possible. Usually 1 tablespoon of faluda is enough for one helping of kulfi.

Page 165 *Coconut pudding (see page 162).*
Previous Page *Blackberry sharbat (see page 172); Yogurt sharbat (see page 172); Kulfi for the princes (see page 171); Banana ice cream (see page 170).*
Left *Cream cheese balls in syrup (see page 154); Batter coils in syrup (see page 155).*

Kulfi
Indian ice cream

*This scrumptious Indian ice cream is not widely known in the West –
it is a very rich dish, of a harder consistency than normal ice cream.
The traditional way of making kulfi is to pour the boiled milk into
long tin moulds with tightly fitting lids. However, I suggest you use
plastic ice cube trays or other suitable containers.*

Atul kela kulfi
Banana ice cream

Serves 6
Preparation time 5 minutes
Cooking and freezing time 2 hours

METRIC/IMPERIAL	AMERICAN
2.25 litres/4 pints creamy milk	10 cups creamy milk
100 g/4 oz sugar	$\frac{1}{2}$ cup sugar
100 g/4 oz flaked almonds	1 cup flaked almonds
100 g/4 oz pistachios, grated	1 cup pistachios, grated
2 ripe bananas, peeled and chopped	2 ripe bananas, peeled and chopped
or 1 teaspoon banana essence	or 1 teaspoon banana extract
1 teaspoon green cardamom seeds,	1 teaspoon green cardamom seeds,
coarsely ground	coarsely ground
2 tablespoons rose water	3 tablespoons rose water

Put the milk in a deep pan and bring to the boil. Add the sugar, almonds and
pistachios and leave to simmer on a low heat until the milk is reduced by half.
Keep stirring from time to time and make sure that the milk does not boil
over.

Remove the pan from the heat, add the banana and cardamom powder and
let the milk cool a little. Find some clean plastic containers, preferably with
lids, and fill them with the milk. Place these containers in the freezer for
about 1 hour, until the milk is frozen.

Take the kulfis from the containers and cut them into round slices. Serve
with a generous sprinkling of the rose water and add a tablespoon of faluda
(see page 169) on each serving, if desired.

Kunwar-kulfi
Kulfi for the princes

Serves 4
Preparation time 10 minutes
Cooking and freezing time 2 hours

METRIC/IMPERIAL	AMERICAN
900 ml/1½ pints creamy milk	3¾ cups creamy milk
225 g/8 oz khoya (see page 29) or condensed milk	½ lb khoya (see page 29) or condensed milk
225 g/8 oz sugar	1 cup sugar
50 g/2 oz flaked almonds	½ cup flaked almonds
25 g/1 oz pistachios, chopped	¼ cup pistachios, chopped
175 g/6 oz peaches, pears and pineapple, fresh or canned, diced	6 oz peaches, pears and pineapple, fresh or canned, diced
1 teaspoon green cardamom powder	1 teaspoon green cardamom powder
4 drops of kewra essence or 2 tablespoons rose water	4 drops of kewra extract or 2 teaspoons rose water
25 g/1 oz pistachios, grated	¼ cup pistachios, grated

Boil the milk and leave to simmer over a low heat for about 20 minutes. Keep stirring, taking care that the milk does not boil over. Still keeping the pan on the heat, add the khoya or condensed milk. If using khoya, add it gradually; add condensed milk in one go. Add the sugar, almonds and pistachios, mix well and leave for a further 15 minutes.

Remove the pan from the heat and let it cool a little. Now add the fruit, having drained off the syrup first, cardamom powder and kewra essence. Mix well with a spoon, taking care not to mash the fruit, and pour into moulds.

Leave the moulds in the freezer for about 1 hour until the kulfi is solid. Transfer to the refrigerator at this stage if it is to be served later. Serve straight from the fridge, as the kulfi will melt quickly if left outside. Decorate it with the grated pistachios.

NOTE Instead of using all the stated fruits above, use only one or two of them or quite different fruits can be used for equally good results. Fruit essence in sufficient quantities can also be used to replace part or all of the fruit.

Sharbat
Cold soft drinks

*It is fashionable in India for the hosts to offer their guests freshly
made sharbats. A glass of freshly made cold sharbat is heavenly in
the early evening breeze after a scorching summer's day.*

Meethi sharbat
Yogurt sharbat

Serves 6
Preparation time 10 minutes

*This is a high-speed cold drink. No sooner have you thought about it,
you can be sipping it.*

METRIC/IMPERIAL	AMERICAN
600 ml/1 pint natural yogurt	2½ cups plain yogurt
4 tablespoons sugar	⅓ cup sugar
1 tablespoon vanilla or other chosen essence	1 tablespoon vanilla or other chosen extract
900 ml/1½ pints ice-cold water	3¾ cups ice-cold water
12 ice cubes, crushed	12 ice cubes, crushed
25 g/1 oz flaked almonds	¼ cup flaked almonds

Mix the yogurt, sugar, essence and water together and mix in the electric
blender. Cover with the lid and leave on high speed for about 1 minute.
Switch off the electric blender and pour the frothy yogurt liquid into six
individual glasses. Add the crushed ice and sprinkle the flaked almonds on
top of each glass before serving.

Phalsa pawan-basera
Blackberry sharbat

Serves 6
Preparation time 9½ hours

METRIC/IMPERIAL	AMERICAN
450 g/1 lb blackberries	1 lb blackberries
900 ml/1½ pints water	3¾ cups water
450 g/1 lb castor sugar	2 cups sugar
12 ice cubes, crushed	12 ice cubes, crushed
6 pineapple rings	6 pineapple rings

Lightly crush the blackberries in a basin and add the water. Leave to soak for 6–8 hours. By this time the water will have drawn all the colour from the blackberries. Mash the water and the blackberries thoroughly.

Strain through a muslin cloth, or press through a fine sieve. Add the sugar and mix thoroughly.

Take out 6 tablespoons of the sharbat, pour it into six ice cube containers and freeze.

Refrigerate the sharbat for at least 1 hour. Pour into 6 tall glasses, add the crushed ice and one phalsa ice cube to each glass. Serve decorated with pineapple rings.

Mohit sharbat
Lemon sharbat

Serves 4
Preparation time 50 minutes

This sharbat is one of the most popular; athletes are particularly partial to it because no other drink is as refreshing after strenuous activity.

METRIC/IMPERIAL	AMERICAN
4 tablespoons lemon juice	$\frac{1}{3}$ cup lemon juice
175 g/6 oz sugar	$\frac{3}{4}$ cup sugar
600 ml/1 pint water	$2\frac{1}{2}$ cups water
4 drops of kewra essence	4 drops of kewra extract
8 ice cubes, crushed	8 ice cubes, crushed
4 round slices of lemon	4 round slices of lemon

Mix the lemon juice, sugar and 1 cup of the water and mix in the electric blender. Add the rest of the water and the kewra essence and blend again for a few seconds more.

Put 4 tablespoons of the sharbat into four ice cube containers and freeze. Refrigerate the sharbat for 30 minutes before serving.

Stir then pour into four glasses. Add crushed ice and one lemon ice cube to each glass and garnish with a slice of lemon.

Index